# 1911
## The Austin Flood

*By Paul W. Heimel*

Knox Books
407 Mill Street
Coudersport PA 16915

ISBN: 978-0-9655824-4-5

*Publisher:*
Knox Books, 407 Mill St., Coudersport PA 16915

*Cover Photo:* Janara Hoppock
*Cover Design/Layout:* Joseph A. Majot
*Photo Editor:* Robert A. Hooftallen

## About The Author

Paul W. Heimel grew up less that a dozen miles from the Austin
Dam and has spent his life in Potter County, Pennsylvania. A
former journalist, he is the author of five history books, including
the critically acclaimed *Eliot Ness: The Real Story* (Cumberland
House Publishing Inc., 2000), which is considered the
authoritative biography of the famous Chicago crimefighter.
Heimel has written dozens of magazine articles and has appeared
on numerous television documentaries and interview programs.

# From the Author

Almost a half-century after the Austin Dam gave way, an eyewitness to the tragedy began the mission of recording the event as thoroughly and accurately as possible. Marie Kathern (Brisbois) Nuschke, a talented writer and dedicated chronicler of local history, was challenged by conflicting and—in many instances—embellished or wholly fictional accounts of the disaster.

Her 40-page paperback, *The Dam That Could Not Break* (1960), was a significant attempt to separate fact from fiction. Nuschke painstakingly studied newspaper reports, cross-referencing them with eyewitness accounts and her own recollections. Her work has been invaluable to dozens of historians, genealogists and others in quest of information about the tragedy of September 30, 1911.

It is with great respect for the Nuschke family that I have picked up the mantle. So much additional information has emerged since *The Dam That Could Not Break* was published. On this 100th anniversary of the Austin flood, the time is right to revisit the events of that terrible day, the twists of fate and tragic missteps that preceded the dam's failure, and the developments that followed.

Only recently did I learn of my own connection to the Austin flood. My great-grandfather, German immigrant Casper W. Heimel (1848-1927), was a town constable in southwestern Pennsylvania who was among those dispatched to Austin to assist in the rescue and recovery, chase down looters, and otherwise keep order in the stricken community.

So many people have influenced this work in one way or another that it's impossible to thank them all. Three of them are deserving of special mention. Joseph A. Majot and I had collaborated with my uncle John H. Graves and others on a newspaper supplement to mark the flood's 75th anniversary in 1986. For the more than two decades that followed, we tossed back and forth the idea of collaborating on an expanded work. The bulk of the research and writing fell to me, but the large volume of material that Joey provided was a treasure trove. Anyone who considers himself better informed about this significant event by reading this book owes him a debt of gratitude.

The daunting task of transforming hundreds of century-old, technically inferior images to quality photographs so effectively displayed in this book blended the skills of my wife, Lugene Heimel, with those of Robert A. Hooftallen and Joseph A. Majot.

I was strongly supported by family members and friends who were pressed into service as researchers, critical reviewers, editors, proofreaders and advisors as I raced the clock to complete the book in time for the flood centennial. Potter County Historical Society, Austin Dam Memorial Association and the E. O. Austin Historical Society opened their archives and could not have been more supportive. My mother, Barbara Fish Heimel; my son, Paul Joseph Heimel; and professional writer Cynthia Heimel offered valuable suggestions down the stretch. Consultants from the National Society of Professional Engineers helped me to comprehend a large volume of technical information on the dam.

This work presented incredible challenges. Newspaper reporters in the early 20th century weren't inclined to allow the truth stand in the way of an attention-grabbing story. Published accounts that would have added more color and sensationalism to this book did not make the cut because they could not be verified. It was also important not to speculate or ascribe motives to the significant figures of the story, but whenever possible to allow them to speak for themselves.

Numerous engineering studies were conducted after the flood. There were disagreements among the professionals over some points, but all concurred about the dam's foundational shortcomings. Therefore, I decided not to dwell on the nuances of the engineers' conflicting findings.

Given the hundreds of historical documents, newspaper stories, court transcripts, interviews and other information woven into this work, development of an index, bibliography or attribution endnotes was impossible. Good faith efforts have been made to attribute any significant passages to their original sources. Similarly, credits for the vast majority of the photos were lacking in the archives of historical museums, the Library of Congress, and the vast personal collections of Joseph A. Majot and Alan Dickerson, upon which this book heavily relied.

———————

As this work reached its final stages, I spent a great deal of time alone in the Freeman Run valley. Hiking through the swampy path on which the wall of water coursed so violently on that fateful September Saturday a century ago. Examining the broken dam from every direction. Climbing its crumbling concrete slopes. Grasping its protruding twisted steel rods— yearning for a connection.

*—Paul W. Heimel, May 2011*

**1911** *The Austin Flood*

# *Table of Contents*

## PART ONE:

# *Table of Contents*

## PART TWO:

### —Eyewitness Accounts—

# Introduction

For countless years, tiny Freeman Run has flowed through the foothills of the Allegheny Mountains in northcentral Pennsylvania, gently tugged along by gravity on its voyage to the Susquehanna River. It's a creek of just a few miles' length, first bubbling forth near the little village of Odin.

On rare occasions it expands to a raging torrent, engorged by storms or snowmelt, only to dwindle to the smallest trickle in the dryness of summer.

Freeman Run has been fouled by lumbermen who tore at the soil as they stripped the virgin timber. It's been bridged, dammed and rechanneled. But, in time, it always cleanses itself of man's excesses. Like an unruly child, it has reacted the most violently when it has been the most restrained. Over time, the river always has its way.

Always.

**1911** *The Austin Flood*

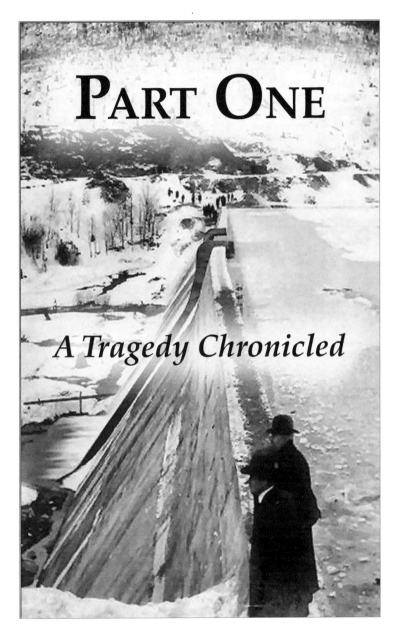

# PART ONE

## *A Tragedy Chronicled*

# 1911 *The Austin Flood*

# 1

## *Too Tough To Die*

*Harry Davis was enjoying a peaceful Saturday outside his hillside home, nodding off in the warmth of the early afternoon sun. He was never sure what jarred him awake—was it the loud crack that echoed down the valley, or the ominous rumble that shook the ground beneath him? No matter. He knew what it meant. He'd half been expecting it.*

*Davis looked up in time to see a massive, thick section of concrete shoot out from near the dam's base. Water roared through the gap. Seconds later, the walls slid and another giant piece fell to the valley floor with a frightening thud. Water gushed relentlessly forward as the dam surrendered to the force. The day had come.*

---

This is the tale of a town that's too tough to die. It's also a lesson in the perils of wishful thinking. Its heroes are easy to identify; the villains less clear and subject to ceaseless speculation and debate.

Northcentral Pennsylvania's Freeman Run valley is a natural paradise of mountains and flourishing vegetation that changes with the seasons. "Potter County: God's Country," is more than a slogan—to some, it has spiritual significance.

Situated in the Appalachian Highland Plateau, the region rode high as lumber barons arrived to hack away at its thick stands of virgin pine and hemlock. Once the giant trees were gone, so was the prosperity. Today, a century later, the area is treasured for its rural character and its year-'round recreational opportunities.

Many who live there are third- or fourth-generation descendants of the immigrants who followed the lumber companies as they sawed their way northward through Pennsylvania. They feel a kinship with the land and take pride in their heritage.

Potter County is unique in that water flows from a divide in three directions – southwest to the Gulf of Mexico via the Allegheny, Ohio and Mississippi rivers; southeast to the Chesapeake Bay via the Susquehanna, or north to Lake Ontario.

This distinction is a result of remarkable changes taking place in the surface of the land area. It was once submerged as ocean bottom, "wrinkled" far above sea level in huge fields, and gradually carved or cut by the power of millions of years of rain. Through it all, the irregular tipped-up layers of sedimentary rock resisted the erosion process, creating the scenic Allegheny Mountains of today.

Native Americans first inhabited the region, drawing their sustenance from the rivers and the surrounding forests. Inevitably, European settlers with a different mentality toward the land began to discover Pennsylvania's great north woods.

Speculators bought up broad expanses after a treaty with the Six Nations of the Iroquois opened much of Pennsylvania's northcentral forests. In 1827, Englishman William Carson cleared a lot and built a log cabin and grist mill where Freeman's Run (later shortened to Freeman) drains a watershed of about 15 square miles, emptying into the First Fork of Sinnemahoning Creek.

The steep terrain made large-scale farming impractical, but the forests were a bounty for timber harvesting, leather tanning and related industries. Other families were drawn by the potential to profit from the rich resources and to enjoy the uncertain serenity of the natural world. They fanned out over the fertile valleys, settling in today's Wharton, Portage and Keating townships and establishing the village of Forest House, now Keating Summit.

---

One of the more notable pioneers was Edward O. Austin, a surveyor and engineer whose family came from Steuben County, New York. He may have been seeking solitude for his family, or perhaps he was motivated by the prospect of prosperity from mineral wealth.

Austin arrived at the junction of Freeman Run's two forks in 1856, about three miles upstream from Carson's settlement in the narrow valley that stretched barely 1,500 feet from side to side. He built a modest log home and established a small farm, the beginning of a community that would later bear his name.

In his diary, E. O. Austin recorded delight with his surroundings: "For me and my family, Freeman's Run is always a ready source of rations. The brookies—they're just the right size for eating and the only limit on how many I take home is how many I decide to keep." Among those who made their way by horse and buggy to test the region's trout waters was Grover Cleveland, the mayor of Buffalo, and later the 27th President of the United States.

Dirt roads were carved through the wilderness to link families in the remote stretches to the community. The Freeman Run Post Office was established, laying the groundwork for what would become one of the longest rural delivery routes in the country.

---

In 1881, P. H. Costello & Company targeted the area where William Carson had settled, then known as North Wharton, for construction of a leather tannery. It was a modest operation—but not for long. Demand for leather was growing as the cities of the Northeast expanded.

Massive vats of pungent tanning liquid required thousands of cords of hemlock bark to create a potion potent enough to stain and chemically preserve the cow hides. Soon, scores were put to work felling trees, stripping the bark or tending to the tanning process. Fueled by the bountiful supply of hemlock, the plant prospered and was eventually reputed to be the largest tannery in the world. Its two tall smokestacks fouled the air for miles, but symbolized progress and prosperity. About 300 men worked in the mammoth three-story, L-shaped factory that daily converted 600 dry hides imported from South America to 1,200 sides of sole leather.

Anyone who was able to work could find a job in the mills and factories or building the railroads. Laborers from Italy, Poland and Ireland were increasingly added to the cultural melting pot that also included British Isles farmers and loggers of New England, Canadian, German and Scandinavian descent.

Some brought their families, while others were single men looking for a fast buck and a good time. Workers also came to the tannery and lumber mills from nearby communities to supplement their farm income with bark peeling, timber cutting and log driving. To honor the community's source of prosperity, residents of North Wharton decided to change the name of their village to Costelloville—later shortened to Costello—with the opening of a post office in 1883.

---

All of the activity attracted the attention of moneyed business speculators, including the ambitious Frank H. Goodyear (1849-1907). Goodyear had abandoned his career as a schoolteacher to chase a dream of fortune in the lumber business. After acquiring tens of thousands of acres of timberlands in the region, the entrepreneur zeroed-in on the Freeman Run valley and purchased another 15,000 acres. He was encouraged by E. O. Austin, who owned most of the acreage in the valley and had used his surveying and engineering skills to lay out a plan for its development. Goodyear's ambition was a perfect match for Austin's dream of a progressive community. Success of his small water-powered lumber mills at Keating Summit and Wharton reinforced his confidence in the region's potential. He built a sawmill in Austin and purchased additional land from E. O. Austin and George Turner, while hacking away at area forests.

Oliver S. Garretson of Buffalo, owner of an extensive hardwood furniture manufacturing empire, soon joined the rush. He purchased thousands of prime acres and announced a plan to build a mill with dual purposes—sawing the hardwood for himself and the hemlock for Goodyear's needs. Garretson's

17

furniture works was a natural complement to the Goodyear operations.

When water conditions were right, lumber and manufactured goods could be sent by rafts to markets downstate. However, the owners were frustrated by the inconsistent flow. Goodyear set out on a plan to link his Sinnemahoning Valley Railroad from Keating Summit, where a spur of the Western New York and Pennsylvania Railroad was located, to his sawmill in Austin and eventually to Costello. That direct line, combined with tram roads and tracks on hogback trails to connect the lumber camps to the mills, would give him a complete rail network to bring in logs for processing and send the finished products to a worldwide market.

Naysayers insisted the train's engines could never climb the high mountains that separated the two communities. Goodyear knew better. He contracted for five modern "stemwinders" that did the job, albeit at a snail's pace on the steeper sections. The first load of logs came from Keating Summit to the Goodyear millpond in November 1885 and the town of Austin was off and running. Soon, Blaisdell Brothers opened a kindling wood factory near the Goodyear mill, using waste products from the mills and hiring anyone who would work, including children.

The railroad extension carried bark from the Goodyear mill south to Alfred Costello's tannery and the finished products of leather and chemicals produced by the tannery back to market.

In 1887, Frank Goodyear recruited his older brother, attorney Charles W. Goodyear, who gave up a lucrative practice with Grover Cleveland to join him. The business prospered under several names, including United Lumber Company, and would become Goodyear Lumber Company in 1900.

———

Austin—fittingly nicknamed "Hemlock City"—was incorporated in 1888 as the growth spree gained even more steam. E. O. Austin was deserving of the honor. He had cleared most of the land and encouraged its development. He had also served as a justice of the peace, a county commissioner, a school director and a Union volunteer in the Civil War.

A newspaper, the *Austin Autograph*, was launched by publisher Harry Caskey with this announcement:

> *Austin is a wonderful town. Two years ago it was a howling wilderness and the post office did not do $65 in business. Now it does $1,200. It has a thousand or more inhabitants, electricity, one of the finest sawmills in the world, and other modern improvements. It's situated in the heart of a 40,000-acre tract of hemlock. Austin is well-provided with stores but it has no newspaper, and I propose to fill the want.*

Homes began to appear up both sides of the steep hills on the community's eastern and western borders, while a business and industrial section continued to expand at the lowest point in the valley. A social structure evolved among the lumbermen who inhabited makeshift camps in the forests outside of town, blending divergent cultures, lifestyles and languages. They worked hard during the day, enduring hot summers and frigid winters, and lived in primitive conditions. Many of their encampments were plagued by dirt, lice, and vermin.

At night, they enjoyed fiddle and accordion tunes, often accompanied by jew's-harps, and played penny-ante poker. Many were physically drained by long work days, so it was early to bed and early to rise.

"Woodhicks" preferred their pay in gold coin. Some packed away earnings to support their families, while others frittered it away on temptations readily available in Austin or Costello. There was no shortage of opportunities for those who leaned toward promiscuity, rowdiness and a live-for-today mentality. Saloons, gambling houses and brothels did a brisk business.

"Pigs-ears," local slang for barrooms, were popular social centers for woodsmen. They also attracted counterfeiters, pickpockets, drifters and outlaws. Ladies of the evening regularly escorted their customers to nearby "hoot houses." Rum and cheap whiskey flowed freely.

Gambling extended beyond the poker games to heavy wagering on bare-knuckle boxing. Disagreements over women, money, ethnicity or just about any other topic were settled with fists. With law enforcement hopelessly outnumbered, "frontier justice" prevailed.

Itinerant evangelists found plenty of candidates for redemption. Some clergy likened Austin and Costello to Sodom and Gomorrah. It was a depiction that offended many of the locals, most of whom eschewed the night life, especially those in class-conscious Costello.

A volunteer fire company, delivering water via bucket brigade, was often outmatched by forest fires that blackened thousands of acres and blanketed the valleys with thick, yellow smoke. These blazes were usually tamed before reaching the towns. An occasional fire was set off by an angry woodhick seeking revenge for a perceived injustice, such as his boss refusing to pay him. From time to time, a property owner would torch a forest stand to open the acreage for natural production of huckleberries in the ruins. Other fires were likely ignited by railroad sparks or lightning.

Austin's business district expanded to occupy the full width of the valley. A main street crossing from east to west and intersecting streets were flanked by mom-and-pop retailers, hotels, a jewelry store, billiard rooms, barber shops and a combination hardware/general store stocking everything from work boots to flour. A passenger train connecting to Keating Summit and Costello passed through town four times a day. Goodyear's loading docks extended for a half-mile. At night the whole valley was ablaze with light from the carbon lamps on the platform. Cock fights, advertised in the *Austin Autograph* as "fights that will out-do any place in western Pennsylvania," drew big crowds. Occasional dog fights were also staged. Musicians merged their talents to form the Hemlock Band, forerunner of the E. O. Austin Band, honoring the man who provided them with a place to practice. In return, his portrait appeared on the face of the bass drum. A school house that opened on the hill was a source of pride and confidence in a growing community.

Austin had its share of infrastructure problems, from dirty and inadequate water supplies that spawned a cholera outbreak, to muddy roads. Main Street was nearly impassable at times, prompting business owners to lay planks over the muck for their customers' convenience.

The 1888 Independence Day celebration provided storytelling fodder for years to come. Amid the revelry, outlaw Tom Kennedy killed one man, wounded another and escaped with his daughters, never to be seen again.

On February 13, 1889, fire struck several downtown buildings. Townspeople called for construction of a public water works in the newly incorporated borough to afford greater fire protection, but after some initial momentum, the project stalled.

Less than three months later, the same storm system that

caused the catastrophic flood in Johnstown, Pennsylvania, struck the state's northern sector. Freeman Run overflowed its banks and caused extensive damage to many homes and businesses. Evangelists declared that God was punishing the town for its promiscuity. Some townspeople agreed, and began praying for redemption. Austin's eight churches—two Catholic and six Protestant—saw increased membership. But for most people, the flood was just another challenge to meet and defeat. They rebuilt and the town rose again.

Austin was tested like never before on August 14, 1890, when another, more devastating, fire roared through the valley. Upwards of 50 buildings, including many businesses on Main Street, were leveled. Within days, the owners started rebuilding, with brick replacing the wooden construction. By Christmas, downtown Austin was back in business.

When Austin debuted on the national census in 1890, its population of 1,670 topped the county seat of Coudersport. Costello was also growing rapidly, fueled by the tannery, and smaller communities were springing up in the region. Goodyear's exponential growth seemed to be limitless. The company's railroad was netting a small fortune while its mill in Austin turned out upwards of 10,000 feet of hemlock per hour, employing 200 in two shifts. Other wood-based businesses prospered, including Davidge Manufacturing Company, producing hubs and veneer, and the Emporium Lumber Company with its crate and wood-chipping factory.

Almost five years to the day of the 1889 flood, on May 29, 1894, raging flood waters swept through Austin again, flattening much of the downtown area and many residences. A few families lost everything and turned to relatives in other towns to take them in.

English immigrants Alice and Nellie Griffiths opened Potter

County's first hospital on Railroad Street. The Griffiths sisters, who were nurses, would soon relocate to the spacious home that was built by Frank Goodyear on School Street. It became Northern Pennsylvania General Hospital, including a training center for nurses from a wide area.

An amateur baseball team enjoyed consistent success against foes from other villages and provided weekend entertainment in the summer. Families often gathered at a picnic grove south of town.

One afternoon in October 1897, local farmer Isaac Mitchell brought a load of hay to town for grocer William Nelson's horses. As he backed his wagon into a livery barn on Railroad Street, it clipped an open gas lamp, igniting the hay. Wind-swept flames spread rapidly through the town. Hot weather and a lingering drought had lowered water supplies and there was little property owners or bucket-brigade volunteers could do. The fire took out 89 homes, two churches, two livery stables, an opera house and several businesses. About one-third of the town was destroyed. Miraculously, there was no loss of life. Once again, Austin rose from the ashes.

The Goodyears' Buffalo and Susquehanna Railroad stretched its web in all directions. Tracks were laid eastward to connect the Freeman Run area to communities such as Cross Fork and Galeton. The northwest extension to Keating Summit continued through Port Allegany in McKean County and eventually to Buffalo. A southern line carried to DuBois and the coalfields in Clarion and Armstrong counties.

---

But time was ticking on the boom towns of northern Pennsylvania. Old-growth trees were replaced by vast expanses of scrub and seedy patches of low-value species. Drifters and even established families began moving westward to hack away at virgin timber to be found in seemingly endless supply in Wisconsin, Michigan and the Pacific Northwest. Others migrated to West Virginia or Louisiana. The Goodyears were turning their attention elsewhere, establishing the Great Southern Lumber Company and the New Orleans and Great Northern Railroad Company while building the largest sawmill in the world at Bogalusa, Louisiana. Austin's economy was in a free fall.

# 2

## *Our Salvation*

No one had a greater stake in the continued vitality of Austin than Frank Elmer Baldwin. A lawyer and bank president, Baldwin had built a mini-empire of real estate and business interests while rising in Republican political circles. He was a descendant of a pioneer family that had settled in New England in the middle of the 17th century. Baldwin opened a law practice in Austin in 1894 and was heir apparent to Edward O. Austin as the town's most influential citizen.

Austin residents turned to Baldwin for help in courting industries that might want to capitalize on a proven workforce. Among his business and political contacts was George C. Bayless, a paper manufacturer from Binghamton, New York. Bayless was the youngest man elected mayor of Binghamton at age 24 in 1887. He became president of the family-owned Bayless Pulp and Paper Company when it was incorporated in 1893. Citing growing business responsibilities, he decided not to seek a second term as mayor in 1891.

George Bayless was intrigued by the suggestion that his

company build a state-of-the-art paper mill to capitalize on the seemingly endless expanses of scrubby pulpwood left behind by the timber cutters in the Austin area. However, his management team drove a hard bargain, demanding that the town deliver a generous package of incentives.

Among the many community leaders who signed on to the campaign to woo Bayless was newspaper publisher Harry Caskey, whose widely circulated publication wielded tremendous influence. The opinionated Caskey also served as president of the Austin Borough Council. Several meetings during the early months of 1900 produced a plan to court the Bayless firm.

Caskey trumpeted the mission in the pages of his *Austin Autograph*:

> *From the time Austin took the place of Freeman Run, this neck o' the woods has been noted for considerable enterprise. We propose to demonstrate to the outside world that traces of that spirit remain in our locality by introducing the greatest industry that has ever dropped into Potter County. Revise your plans and mark Austin as a permanent and important place in Potter County. We guarantee more business here and more work for the laboring class than any two towns in the county.*

Dozens of business leaders and other citizens signed petitions agreeing to offer inducements to Bayless Pulp and Paper Company that included:

- selection from among three large tracts of real estate and demolition of any structures currently occupying the property;

- construction of an earthen dam to impound upwards of 50 million gallons of water from Freeman Run;

- agreement from an upstream farmer to not pollute the stream or impede its flow from his grist mill in the village of Odin;

- stone quarries from which building foundation material could be obtained;

- homes for employees who move to Austin to work for Bayless;

- a railroad siding and right-of-way to accommodate incoming raw materials and outgoing finished products from the mill;

- drilling of three wells to help supply the mill's water needs;

- a connection and contract with a private water company to service sprinkler equipment and hydrants.

Many local Democrats, led by businessman William Nelson, were leery of the Bayless plan. To them, it symbolized a major corporation exploiting a needy town for cheap labor. Nelson owned numerous properties in Austin and was considered the quintessential populist. He had been elected Potter County Register of Wills and Recorder of Deeds in 1899 as the champion of the common man, keeping a check on what he described as a corrupt Republican establishment that was beholden to business interests.

To make the deal more palatable to skeptics, supporters emphasized the importance of the new dam as a ready source of water for fire protection. Opposition faded and the majority of the town's business owners and citizens contributed money for land acquisition. There were more than 125 donors, with pledges ranging from $5.00 to $500. Still, supporters were unable to raise enough capital to build the dam, so they turned to the taxpayers. Upwards of 90 percent of Austin's citizens signed their consent to fund the plan with public monies.

Harry Caskey dismissed the critics—"those who always oppose everything"—in his newspaper columns. He pointed out that the project would roughly double the town's tax base and create much-needed jobs as the lumber companies continued their exodus. An agreement was signed between Austin Borough and Bayless Pulp and Paper Company on June 6, 1900, and construction began immediately.

Stone masons, brick layers, carpenters and other laborers were assembled to dig trenches and haul stones, bricks and lumber to a site located deep in the valley north of town. A small reservoir was established on the western hillside as a supplemental water source.

Bayless agreed to invest $600,000 for buildings and equipment that included a five-story-high digester, large engines, boilers and a wood chipper capable of processing 100 cords of four-foot slabs every 10 hours. The mill was projected to crank out about 50 tons of paper daily.

A high-production paper mill required an immense amount of electricity, water and steam power to grind the wood and convert it from pulp to paper. In winter, Freeman Run was subject to freezing, and in late summer it ran very low. The town-financed dam was designed to collect water during higher flows and allow the Bayless company to draw it down as needed by the mill.

Little in the way of engineering was employed to create the 380-foot-long, 25-foot-high structure. Construction began with a wall built of a rubble stone, tapered from five and one-half feet thick at the bottom and 18 inches at the top. Unpacked earth slopes were then laid on both downstream and upstream sides. A lake of about 25 million gallons formed between the two steep hills that rose 500 feet above the valley floor. Water was fed to the mill through pipes running down the ravine.

Bayless obtained most of his stock from the region's hemlock sawmills. With the Goodyear Company phasing out its operations, Bayless was able to bring aboard skilled laborers with a proven work ethic. By the time Goodyear made its last purchase of timber in Potter County in March 1902, Bayless had 200 people working and a healthy $9,000 monthly payroll.

Jobs from the paper mill filled many of the empty houses and fueled the construction of others. Austin now extended in three directions, with Main Street crossing the valley from mountain to mountain. Bayless workers' residences could be found mostly along Turner, Railroad and Rukgaber streets, running parallel to Freeman Run and the railroad tracks.

A sense of order began to emerge in the "new" Austin. Visionaries worked to build a community anchored on a more lasting foundation of diverse industry, churches, schools, a hospital, a bank, passenger rail service, community facilities and families who planned to stay. Expansion east of Main Street was blocked by the steep terrain, so some homes were built on a "terrace" overlooking the business district. There was considerable development on the west end of Main Street, where the land is flatter. A road through the western divide followed the railroad grade to another lumbering settlement, Keating Summit, and was dotted with clearings and modest homes.

South of Main Street were the scaled-down Goodyear mills and the Standard Wood Company kindling factory, with their narrow piles of lumber stretching down the valley for upwards of a mile. Farther to the south was the Emporium Lumber Company mill and its own stacked lumber.

As the new century dawned, the ethnic diversity broadened to include more Polish, Irish and Scandinavian mill workers, as well as French-Canadian, Slovenian and Austrian wood cutters. A few African-Americans worked as teamsters in the liveries.

Among additions to the commercial center were a Chinese laundry known as Lee Fong's, and two clothing stores operated by Jewish families, Saul Deisches' on the south side near Costello Avenue and Borowsky's Dry Goods farther west along Main Street. They were soon joined by Frank Rosenbloom, a 26-year-old Lithuanian Jew who had been peddling jewelry and other merchandise in the lumber camps around Austin. He partnered with a Main Street furniture dealer, Frank Sykes, to open a clothing and shoe store next to the Sykes brothers' dry goods and furniture store.

"It galls me that some quasi-historians make it sound as if Austin was one big barroom and bordello and that's all there was," said Bob Currin, who has devoted much of his life tending to the affairs and archives of the Potter County Historical Society. "These people had the same concerns, the same pride, and the same willingness to work for their community as other people did."

# 3

## *False Economy*

Much of the town's vitality was pegged to Bayless Pulp and Paper Company. Conditions inside the mill were dirty, loud, smelly and oftentimes hot and humid. Grinding gears, belts and pulleys, razor-sharp chippers, beater machines, fast-spinning heavy rollers and powerful engines were a constant danger. Workers put in long hours of physically demanding work for low pay.

As the company's reputation grew, so did demand for its products. The combined output of mills in Austin, Binghamton and Quebec made Bayless the world's largest manufacturer of some varieties of paper.

While Freeman Run provided the lifeblood of the mill, it was afforded little respect in return. Discharges of bleach, sodium sulfite and caustic soda sometimes overwhelmed the creek. Residents downstream complained of fish kills and offensive odors. Farmers were forced to fence their cattle away from the river. However, efforts to compel the company to reduce its discharges were met with stiff resistance, both from

Bayless and from Austin businessmen who had grown dependent on the mill.

Austinites came to refer to Freeman Run below the mill as "the acid creek." One described it as "a noxious, disgusting waste dump for the paper mill . . . It was true to its name in odor and in the variety of colors in the creek water that ran from the mill, depending on the type of paper being manufactured that day."

A group of citizens sued, claiming the mill was creating a public nuisance, but Judge John Ormerod ruled in Bayless's favor. He found that, as offensive as the discharges were, they did not pose a health threat to humans.

A fire on November 1, 1904, traced to dust building up in the registers, destroyed the primary school and damaged the adjacent high school. Water scarcity hampered the firemen trying to save the building. Volunteer firefighters pointed out that as long as the Goodyear and Bayless business interests continued to divert much of the water flowing in Freeman Run, there could be no viable public water works. After a prolonged legal battle, the two companies were ordered to loosen their hold on the water sources and allow the borough to build a system that would bring its citizens clean, safe water and a more functional fire department.

Before the timber was stripped from the hillsides, the roots held rain waters for more gradual release and shaded the soil to limit evaporation. Without the trees, rainfall glided into the valley and flowed southward at levels that were beyond the dam's capacity to capture it. The structure's downstream slope was gradually being washed away as water overpowered the spillway. Bayless vowed to reinforce it once he had recouped more of his firm's investment in the mill.

During the late summer, reduced water flows and

evaporation caused the lake to vanish, forcing Bayless to cut his output at the very time demand for his product was rising. Company profits were marginal, but opportunity abounded if only the water shortage could be solved. Bayless huddled with his advisors. He had three options: he could operate seasonally; he could close his plant and reopen at a location with greater water supplies, or he could build a bigger dam to create a deeper lake.

Bayless sought the counsel of several experts. One engineer, H. L. Coburn, submitted a plan that the company dismissed as too expensive. Documentation of his recommendation is lacking, but Coburn was clearly disturbed that Bayless rejected it.

"The whole spirit which prevailed at this time was one of saving every possible dollar of first cost, a particularly striking example of false economy," Coburn told the Association of Engineering Societies. "If there is any class of structure in which the desire to save a few dollars of first cost is likely to result in ultimate financial loss — to say nothing of danger to life — than dams, I do not know it. To my mind, there can be no justification for skimping on any reinforced concrete structure, whether a dam or a building."

Bayless eventually turned to T. Chalkley Hatton, an engineer from Wilmington, Delaware, who was widely respected. An initial plan involved tapping into the plentiful water resources that could be found farther down the Sinnemahoning Creek valley. Water from the confluence of stream's East Fork and First Fork in the village of Wharton would be pumped back upstream to the paper mill. This would have solved the water shortage, but the men concluded that building and maintaining the 14- or 16-inch pipeline of roughly nine miles would be more expensive than building a taller dam.

# 1911 *The Austin Flood*

In January 1909, Bayless gave Hatton the go-ahead to design a concrete dam and asked him to target groundbreaking for April 1 at the latest.

Archived at the Potter County Historical Society museum in Coudersport is a series of correspondence between Bayless and Hatton that reveals the testy relationship that developed between them. These letters also document the corners that were cut to trim costs and expedite construction of the dam. The exchange, while technical in many respects, provides a valuable glimpse into the dynamics that were at play. Excerpts are chronologically interspersed throughout this chapter.

**Hatton, February 8**: *If you want to start construction by April First, we must hustle to get the preliminary plans completed, and of course before doing this it seems necessary to have a careful study made of the site of the dam, and the reservoir it will make. This survey should include an investigation of the quality of the foundation to be encountered and its probable depth, also the topography to determine the proper and most economical height of the dam. I will at once begin a study of your suggestions with a view of designing the cheapest cross-section possible commensurate with safety.*

The first setback came when Bayless attempted to secure land for the new dam and its reservoir. The valley north of the mill and its enormous wood yard was divided into small farms and building lots. At least five property owners would need to sell in order for the plan to move forward. One of them, identified only as "McIntyre" in correspondence, stubbornly refused the Bayless firm's offer to purchase his acreage at a highly inflated price, so Hatton was directed to investigate alternative sites or resurrect the plan to build the pipeline from

Wharton.

However, for reasons that are unclear – the threat of eminent domain may have been a factor—Frank Baldwin and mill superintendent Fred Hamlin were able to persuade the stubborn landowner to sell. Bayless now had all of the property he would need for the dam, the water impoundment, hillside quarries to provide building materials, and a new access road on the western hillside.

**Bayless, February 15**: *When you arrive in Austin, we will show you in the quarries open on the side the way the rock runs throughout the whole country and will have men dig holes in the bottom to show you how the rock lays. The rock is just the same in one place as in another, very shelly on the outside but gets more firm down five or six feet. We could erect a dam at the lower edge of our own land and build it high enough to flood over the top of our present dam to the height of 12 to 14 feet.*

Townspeople grew excited as the word spread about the mission of three well-dressed men who carried sketches, charts and measuring tools over the snowy wasteland and scrub timber of the valley above the paper mill. Hatton, his brother, and his assistant, engineer W. G. Rommell, spent several days inspecting the site. Their mission was to create a water supply that would allow Bayless to operate the mill non-stop and boost production by about 60 percent, to 80 tons per day. That would require roughly 4 million gallons of water daily.

The men obtained United States Weather Bureau precipitation data for the past decade. They then returned to Delaware to work on a plan that was delivered to George Bayless on March 9. It recommended a 58.5-foot-high concrete dam at a site about a quarter-mile below the earthen dam. To save money on the horizontal measures, the engineering team selected a site where the valley narrowed slightly, about one mile upstream from the Bayless mill.

**Hatton, March 9**: *I investigated the underlying strata, so far as able within the time I could devote, and am of the opinion that a good bed of rock for the support of a dam can be secured. From the evidence, however, the rock cannot be obtained within six feet of the surface of the valley. It will most likely be between 12 and 15 feet, whereas on the sides good rock can be met at from 6 to 12 feet below the surface. In building a high dam it is quite necessary to secure as firm rock as possible for the purpose of preventing leakage and to support the excessive weight. The few feet of broken, shelly rock which tops the heavier stratas throughout the valley would not support such a weight. To maintain this weight without crushing, good solid rock is necessary. I had a hole dug about 5-1/2 feet deep in the middle of the valley but did not strike rock, nor any evidence of it. What was struck was a closely packed glacial drift such as might be expected in the valley and I am of the opinion that a large amount of the leakage from your present dam is due to its being built on this drift which will not hold water. In fact, in carefully examining the valley immediately below the dam I detected numerous bubbling springs, indicating the water was being forced through the ground with greater pressure than that due to natural springs.*

Bayless studied the recommendation and asked for cost estimates, adding, "We want to put in as cheap a dam as we can and have it safe, and if this does not run into too much money, we will probably go ahead with the matter at once."

One issue over which the men locked horns was Hatton's recommendation of a gate mechanism—valves, screens, channel walls, cast iron blow-off and supply pipe through the dam to draw off the water in case of emergency. Bayless balked at the $3,755 cost and Hatton acquiesced.

**Bayless, March 29**: *I had a meeting of our directors and they seemed unwilling to expend more than about $85,000, so we will have to cut every possible corner. Can we decrease the cost of the filter or screening proposition (gate mechanism) for leading the water down from the dam to the mill, and for cleaning out? Please do everything you can to reduce the cost of this construction, making it safe of course at the same time.*

**Hatton, March 30**: *Regarding cutting corners on the work, I assure you I am in perfect accord with your desire, and to do this I have gone over and over my plans, having made three complete sets to date, and cut each section down a little until I have not a yard more material of any kind than I can do without in order to make it work safe. Yes, I can cut the gate house out entirely, and put the 36-foot cast iron pipe through the dam with screen chamber on the upper end. This will cut off $1,800 from the estimate. It is my purpose to keep the cost of this dam down to its lowest point, but I must insist, so long as I am consulted by you, upon its being safe both now and hereafter, not only for your safety but for my own reputation as an engineer.*

Time and time again, Bayless pressured Hatton to find ways to lessen expenses in his choices of cement, pipes, steel rods and other supplies at minimal cost. Once these issues were resolved, a contract was signed with C. J. Brintnall and Company, of Binghamton, New York, for construction of the dam at a fee of 10 percent over its actual cost. Charles J. Brintnall was a former railroad builder from New Jersey whose company had recently completed two railroad tunnels and three bridges. Brintnall would not live to see the dam completed. He was killed in a car crash in June 1909 at Owego, New York.

Ever the booster, the *Autograph's* Caskey heralded news of the dam: "It will require an immense amount of machinery and material—six or seven months and a large crew of men working day and night to finish the job. This new dam will insure the plant will run four months without even a drop of new water coming into the reservoir. Surely, a new dam will mean greater prosperity to a community stinging from the fading Big Timber."

The dam was to be 544 feet long, with a width of 30 feet on the base and a maximum height of 51 feet. Width at the top would be two and one-half feet. Its upstream face would be vertical, with the downstream face pitched at an angle of about 36 degrees. The slope was to commence about 12 feet from the top, where the thickness was about six feet, depending on earth backing as a portion of its resistance. Hatton envisioned that it would impound approximately 260 million gallons of water, at a depth of 40 feet.

For vertical reinforcement, the blueprints called for twisted steel rods 25 feet long and 1.25 inches in diameter, five feet inside of the upstream face. Wider steel rods were to be placed horizontally and vertically in the upper 12 feet of the dam. Holes would then be drilled into the foundation rock from five to eight feet deep and steel rods with expansion-bolt heads placed into these holes, which would then be grouted. The top 12 feet of the dam would be reinforced with one-half inch steel rods spaced two feet vertically and four feet horizontally to prevent cracking.

A "concrete gravity dam" uses the weight of the structure as its main source of strength. A cross-section resembles a triangle. Water in the upstream reservoir pushes horizontally against the dam, and the weight of the dam pushes downward to counteract the water pressure. Concrete is not particularly strong in tension when it is pulled or stretched, but it is very strong in compression.

This type of dam was designed for situations where the base of the dam rested on solid rock with no chance for water to seep underneath. Despite Hatton's strong recommendation for a four-foot-deep cutoff wall on the upstream side of the dam to reduce the risk of infiltration, Bayless refused.

Brintnall's crew began construction on May 8, joined by another group of laborers, mostly Italian immigrants. These workers brought their own new element to the community's diverse population. The presence of the dam builders caused some unease in Austin, where the locals found their accents, personalities and personal habits curious.

Like the woodsmen before them, the dam workers demanded to be paid in gold. That created security concerns, especially at the overcrowded Austin Post Office, where labor organizer, or "padrone," Jesus Faronne's crew brought the gold in exchange for money orders sent back to Italy.

Tensions rose at the construction site when the workers threatened to strike unless they were given a raise of 15 cents to a new wage of $1.35 per day. Brintnall conceded, raising George Bayless's ire. "So long as they have given in to these Italians, by the time the work is underway there will be another strike and probably they would be willing to make another advance, as it means nothing to them but rather a gain," Bayless wrote.

Just two weeks passed before Hatton was raising red flags about the geologic features and making another strong pitch for the upstream cutoff wall.

**Hatton, May 21**: *I found upon investigation while at Austin that we had struck a very good stratum of rock at a depth of about eight feet below the natural surface of the ground and so I directed that this be used for the permanent foundation for the dam, but that the stratum was not sufficiently thick to allow us to use it for the cutoff wall, and that this cutoff wall would have to be put down deeper. The indications are that it may have to go three or four feet below the stratum we are building the concrete on.*

**Bayless, May 24**: *I am sorry that the rock you found at eight feet below the natural surface of the ground was not sufficiently thick so as to make a cutoff wall unnecessary. This is an expensive part of the job and I am anxious to hold the price down to the minimum cost wherever we can and make the same secure.*

The strata of the entire valley was soft sandstone interspersed with layers of clay and shale that was carried down into the bedrock. The sandstone was in horizontal layers running from eight inches to three feet thick. Between these layers were beds of shale and disintegrated sandstone topped with five to eight feet of earth and tightly compacted gravel deposited over the centuries from the washings of the side hills.

Digging deeper meant spending money and delaying completion. Despite his misgivings, Hatton eventually yielded to Bayless's pressure.

# 4

# *The Best Of Times*

To reduce costs, the Bayless dam was constructed of "cyclopean masonry"—quarry stones one-half to two and one-half cubic yards each, embedded in wet concrete, with larger boulders used near the bottom.

Quarries were opened at either end of the dam to supply twin mixing plants. Local sandstone was crushed and screened to provide material for the concrete. Construction was done in "lifts" as the dam was raised section by section. The steps dovetailed both horizontally and vertically.

Austin's townspeople regularly made the trek to witness the progress. The work was hard and fast-paced, performed rain or shine. Concrete was chuted down from the sides at the dam's flanks and shoveled into place. To reach the middle sections, a cableway that could carry buckets of material to workers was stretched across the valley.

In early July, Bayless inspected the work and complained that engineer Rommel was directing workers to build three-foot-high pens with six-inch concrete layers in the trench.

## 1911 *The Austin Flood*

Hatton was clearly miffed.

**Bayless, July 3**: *I do not see the use or excuse for doing the work in this way. It is a very difficult matter to get the stone over into these pens and little will be accomplished. The work will drag and be very expensive. I would like to have this sort of thing cut out.*

**Hatton, July 12**: *I beg to advise you that Mr. Rommel is carrying out my directions, given with a view of securing not only the monolithic concrete, but providing against contraction and expansion cracks and subsequent leaking of this dam. I take it that you have employed me for the purpose of getting the advantage of my knowledge to insure this dam against subsequent fracture and leakage. As your consulting engineer, I feel a professional responsibility in having this work properly carried out, and while I am anxious to have the dam constructed in the shortest possible space of time, and with the least cost, yet I must insist upon it being built in a safe way. Of course, you are having this dam built and are paying for it and if I am constructing it in any way which is objectionable to you, and you will write me a letter directing me to build it in a contrary way, I would, of course, follow your directions, but the responsibility is then taken from my shoulders and put upon yours. I have during my practice built a great many dams and so far I have never had a failure. At this time in my professional career I am rather anxious not to have one, for if this dam fails I might as well go out of business.*

The need for a dam was underscored by the exceptionally hot weather of 1909. Newspaper accounts called the drought "unprecedented." Forest fires were an almost daily occurrence. But it was another blaze of disastrous proportions that drew the public's attention to Austin. On July 14, an overheated oven triggered a fire in a bakery on Main Street sometime around 3:30 am. It spread rapidly and, within two hours, eight downtown wooden and brick buildings were gutted or destroyed. For some victims, this was the third destructive fire. And, to make matters worse, insurance coverage was minimal as a result of the town's high risk.

Undaunted, business owners proceeded to rebuild, adhering to a new borough ordinance requiring that buildings be constructed of brick. All of the construction work in town and the large force of men working on the dam made Austin the region's hub of activity. Work began on an earthen bank on the upstream side of the dam, sloping down from a high point of 27 feet tall. It was composed of disintegrated shale, clay and some loam, free from large stones and carefully compacted. An 18-inch pipe was laid from the base of the dam to the paper mill to provide a steady flow of water.

Labor unrest at the Bayless Pulp and Paper mill in September spilled over to the dam site. Striking workers demanded that daily wages be increased from $1.50 to $1.75. Two dozen employees broke ranks and reported for work at the dam. Another 30 workers were called in under the direction of a Hungarian crew boss in St. Marys, about 40 miles to the southwest.

Things got ugly when 175 strikers swooped down and drove off the workers by throwing stones and wielding clubs. Potter County Sheriff A. G. Kenneda deputized eight men and proceeded toward Austin, where his group met up with more than a dozen "special police" that mill superintendent Fred Hamlin and Austin Police Chief Daniel Baker, who was the

Bayless plant foreman, were able to muster.

"Quite a number from Coudersport went to Austin to watch the proceedings of the day," the *Potter Enterprise* reported. "Austin people are much excited over the status of affairs as the foreigners are in an ugly mood, no doubt urged on by some outside labor agitator among their number."

A week later, the newspaper reported that the strike was resolved without any physical altercation: "Everything is now quiet except the hum of the work being done by the bunch of foreigners that went on a strike. After several of the ringleaders in the strike had been chased by the deputies and brought to the borough bastile, the men decided that they were up against it and quieted down. Most of them returned to work the next morning when the whistle sounded."

Cold weather began to hamper the dam's construction as October arrived. Workers covered the freshly poured concrete each evening to protect it from an overnight frost that could compromise its integrity and slow the morning work shift.

With time running out, Hatton took another shot at persuading Bayless to install an accessible drain pipe.

**Hatton, October 1:** *I am not entirely satisfied with the absence of a proper valve on the outer end of the cleanout pipe. While I understand that you do not anticipate using this pipe, still there are times likely to arise in all high dams when for safety of the structure it may be desirable to open up the cleanout pipe and release the pressure. If you had a valve to do this, it could easily be done; whereas with a cap over the pipe, it would be quite impossible to take this cap off with the pressure against it. I still feel that a 36-inch valve should be placed on the end of this cleanout pipe.*

**Bayless, October 2**: *I do not think at the present time we will put a 36-inch valve on the front side of the dam for controlling the water pipe. We have a cap made for the pipe and it will be sufficient at least for the present.*

As the dam neared completion, the division between the men widened.

**Hatton, November 1**: *Last night I received a telegram from Mr. Rommel, stating you desired to raise the spillway for the dam two feet. I have made a computation of the structure, and I find that it would be dangerous to the stability of the structure to increase the height of the water above what we have provided. I, therefore, cannot make any changes to the dam, unless you instruct me to do so over your written signature, thus relieving me of all responsibility.*

**Bayless, November 2**: *From your letter I judge that the dam is hardly safe at the point we expect to carry the water. If this is the situation, it is your fault that it was built this way. We expected there was a good factor of safety in this dam and that the raising of the water a foot or two would not make any particular difference. It was never our intention to put up at Austin a dam relative to the safety of which there could be any question. The original plan as I understood it was that the dam was to be absolutely safe when we had three feet of splash boards in the spillway which would bring the water up to 44 feet. A few weeks ago we thought it best to put two feet more on top of the dam and as I understand you, this was provided for, and at the same time we raised the spillway two feet. I do not see any reason why we cannot raise the* *spillway two feet more, as this would not necessitate using such high flash boards. If there was any question about the strength of the structure, why did we not reinforce the middle third, or why do we not now raise the sides of the intake on the upstream side, and we can then fill in behind the dam with dirt eight or ten feet higher so as to make the proposition secure?*

**Hatton, November 6**: *If you expect to keep adding to the height of the dam, so as to raise the height of the water without correspondingly broadening its base, of course the dam will be unsafe, but how its failure from this cause could possibly be my fault, I fail to see. When I first presented my plans to you for this dam, they provided for a dam five feet thick at top, and 33.1 feet at ground level, with 11 feet depth of foundation. This provided for the spillway to be 41 feet above ordinary level of ground. After going over the whole matter with you, at your office, you insisted upon my cutting down the work so as to get it within a total cost of $85,000, as you assured me that was the maximum amount your directors would permit to be expended upon the project. I, therefore, cut the thickness of the top to two feet, the thickness of the bottom to 30 feet, made the foundation eight feet, and in order to make up for this added reinforcement at bottom to prevent overturning, should the water get under the foundation, and added an embankment on the upstream side. I cut the construction of the dam down to the lowest safe limit to meet your expenditure, and at the same time to make it safe within the duty agreed upon. Now, however, after the dam is almost completed, you want to raise the water two feet, which adds largely to its duty, and you infer that* *it is my fault that this cannot be done. I submit to your sense of fairness if this inference is just. My assistant engineer advised me a few weeks ago that you directed him to raise the free board two feet, but no mention was made of the spillway being raised until last week, when you wrote a letter to Mr. Hamlin, at the bottom of which you added in ink, instructions to raise the spillway two feet. This letter was shown to me when I was in Austin this week. Ordinarily such instructions are taken up with your consulting engineer, who is given the opportunity of advising you before a change of plan is authorized, but in the Austin work all directions for changes have been given without the consulting engineer knowing anything about it. There is no need of my suggesting that the building of high dams is a work which requires the utmost care, both in design and in construction. I have been careful in my design, and everyone connected with the work has been careful in the construction, and I am quite sure your dam is perfectly safe for the duty for which it was designed. But it is not usual to change the duty after the dam is practically built, and I feel sure you will see the matter in the same light when you carefully consider it. I hope you will not insist on having your directions for raising this spillway two feet, carried out.*

**Bayless, November 8**: *We do not expect to keep on adding to the height of the dam but we are anxious to carry in the dam every foot of water possible and have the proposition a safe one. Your first plans provided for a larger expenditure than we cared to make and you knew at the time that we were obliged to confine our expenditures to about $85,000, and that we wanted to get*

47

*in a dam that would carry every foot of water possible
for this sum and carry it safely. I understood that the top
of the spillway on your plan was four feet below the top
of the dam and that we could use three feet of splash
boards in the spillway provided by so doing the water did
not overflow the entire length of the dam. In other words,
that the one foot of 50 feet long would take care of the
water. I assumed that the dam would hold, if it was in
time of flood filled to the top of the walls with water. If
this is the case, we might as well make the spillway two
feet deep instead of four feet, and not provide for any
splash boards. In other words, make the dam as high as it
is in the plans and carry the spillway up within two feet
of the top. In regard to instructions given to Mr. Hamlin,
he is the only way we have to get anything done on the
dam. Mr. Hamlin is of course expected to report the matter
to your assistant and he to you. I do not intend to ask you
to do the impossible but I want to put behind the dam
every foot of water it will carry, and I would like to have
your instructions given to Rommel to build that spillway
just as high as it is safe to build it without putting on any
flash boards.*

After all of the turmoil, the Brintnall crew's foreman
declared that work on the dam was completed just before
Thanksgiving. An itemized bill reflected 15,780 cubic yards
of concrete, 7,925 cubic yards of excavation in foundations,
and 6,360 cubic yards of embankment. Construction cost came
in at $71,821. Counting payments to Hatton and Brintnall &
Company, the total cost was approximately $86,000.

A diversion ditch that channeled Freeman Run away from
the construction zone was filled in and water began to pool at

the base of the dam. Townspeople made a game out of predicting how fast the water level would rise. Community leaders believed the lake that would form behind the dam would one day attract the upper crust of outdoor recreation enthusiasts, making Austin a resort community.

The dam symbolized confidence in the future, prosperity and the town's dogged determination to recover from the adversity of fires, floods and economic recession. There would always be water to turn the mill's wheel. Pulp would roll in from an ever-widening geographic circle to be mashed to its basic elements and converted to paper. And demand for the Bayless product was rising with early 20th century population growth and advances in literacy. Other towns that shrank as the lumbering boom faded would look upon Austin with envy.

Hatton arrived to inspect the dam and reported to Bayless that, although it was "a very excellent piece of work," he remained uneasy.

**Hatton, November 26**: *I feel that it is my duty to again call your attention to this point. There is no convenient way provided for relieving the dam of an unexpected and unlooked-for flood. You may remember that when we went over the original design for this dam, a gate house with sluice gate was provided, by which the dam could be emptied, through a 36-inch cleanout pipe, or the pressure could be relieved by this pipe, through this valve. In order to cut down the expense, however, the gate house was eliminated, and you agreed to put in a plug upon the outer end of the cleanout pipe, which could be taken off in case of necessity. I had not seen this plug until my last visit to Austin, when I examined it carefully and I believe that it* *will be absolutely useless for the purpose of relieving the dam of any excess pressure due to flood, because at that time it will be absolutely impossible for anybody to take this plug off, as at such a time the water would be running over the spillway, immediately over this plug, and it would be impossible for anybody to get at it. So I believe that for the safety of the dam, in the case of an extreme flood, it would be far better to have a valve placed at the outer end of the blowoff pipe, with the stern of the valve extended four or five feet above the spillway, so that the operator of the valve may stand upon the bridge while opening or closing the valve. Now I don't want to be misunderstood that I have any fear whatever of the failure of the dam, under not only ordinary conditions, but under conditions which have heretofore existed in this watershed. But as I have written before, there are unlooked-for floods which are likely to occur in any watershed, and it is just for these occasions that blowoff pipes, with proper regulations, are built into dams. I wish you would reconsider this matter carefully. It seems to me that inasmuch as the cost of the dam, so far as I am now able to state, has been within our estimates, that the installation of this valve would not be a hardship to you. I want to assure you that we have all tried, not only to build a good piece of work, but to build it as cheaply as possible, and with the utmost dispatch, and so far as I have been able to observe, everyone in authority, connected with the work, including your superintendent at the mill, has done his utmost to this end.*

Bayless was in Canada and did not respond to Hatton's letter for more than two weeks. In the meantime, on December 1,

1909, even before the lake had fully formed, signs of structural instability had surfaced. A crack appeared, running from the breast of the dam vertically to the base. It measured about one-sixteenth of an inch, some 50 feet west of the midpoint.

**Bayless, December 11**: *I note your suggestion in regard to the relief pipe. There certainly should be some way so that we could if necessary open up the 36-inch cleanout pipe. We do not get very heavy floods at Austin. I have seen just one which was sort of a cloudburst and from an empty dam filled the old dam to overflowing in about an hour. This came up suddenly one afternoon as we were about shutting down through lack of water, and in a very short space of time, we had as much of a flood as ever occurred at Austin insofar as we can ascertain, and I think that the present spillway would take care of the water in the head. However, I am anxious to have it safe in every way. I am very glad to note that the totals are within your estimate. I thought they would overrun same. I believe that everyone engaged in the erection of the dam has done his level best to build a good, safe piece of work and without undue expense.*

By the end of the month, a second crack could be seen 40 feet east of the center. Bayless and his engineers explained that these small fissures were the result of temperature-related contraction of the concrete and were not related to the stability of the structure.

That explanation was greeted with skepticism by two outspoken critics, Sarah Willetts and William Nelson. They were sometimes mocked for their repeated references to the dam's instability. Most took comfort in the notion that, if the dam failed, the water would spread out over the valley and be nothing but a nuisance when it reached Austin some two miles downstream.

The Bayless company diverted attention from the dam by announcing that it had signed contracts to manufacture a line of white sulphite paper that would require expansion of the mill. Bayless was also negotiating with buyers of a new line of kraft paper. There was one critical problem, however. The new product lines would more than double the mill's water demands.

# 5

## *'Nothing Has Been Done'*

Rain and melting snow from a mid-winter thaw caused the lake to rise rapidly, putting incredible pressure on the dam and raising doubts about its integrity. Water could be seen dribbling through the cracks. Of greater concern was discovery of leakage bubbling up from the ground just below its base.

On Saturday, January 21, 1910, water began pouring over the spillway. The next day, a massive slice of earth from the eastern slope slid into the valley, allowing some water to slip around the side of the structure. Greater volumes could be seen percolating up from the ground, 15 to 50 feet below the toe of the dam.

Superintendent Hamlin and one of his employees, Joseph McKinney, rode up to the dam with horse and wagon and were alarmed to discover that the two-month-old structure had bowed almost three feet at the top center. The lake's ice surface, which had previously been flush with the dam, was now separated from it. Six vertical cracks could clearly be seen across the face of the dam.

Convinced that disaster was imminent, the men raced southward to warn Austin. They stopped at the home of Oscar Clafflin, at the upper end of the paper mill's wood yard. "Mr. Hamlin came down to my house that morning, and he said, 'For God's sake, move out—the dam is breaking!',", Clafflin said. "So I moved my furniture up on the hill with the exception of the cook stove and little stuff."

Hamlin and McKinney continued into town. Many took the threat seriously, moving their belongings upstairs and ushering their children and pets indoors. Some took refuge on the hillsides. Merchants closed up shop and schools dismissed their students. A sizable number of townspeople professed faith in the structure and went about their business. Joseph McKinney continued on to his house and joined his wife, Olive, in rounding up the couple's six children and as many possessions as they could carry to higher ground.

The dam site echoed with the gurgling and splashing of water escaping its confinement and the eerie and ominous sounds of a concrete structure that was overstressed. As the hours passed, most of those who fled returned to the valley. But many remained fearful and were welcomed into the homes of relatives or neighbors on the hillsides. They were mocked by those who had stayed put.

Curious Austin residents flocked to the dam to look on from the safety of the hillsides. A. C. Sylvius, a state forester, was among them. " I thought it was going to break," Sylvius said. "I observed very serious defects—perpendicular crevices or fissures. I recall three large ones, probably six inches wide. I saw that the dam had moved, because there was a curve in it. Before there was any water in it, it had been straight across the front."

Harry Davis, a retired Buffalo and Susquehanna Railroad

engineer who lived in the home directly above the dam on the eastern hillside, said he heard an unusual sound coming from the valley in the wee hours of the morning on Sunday. He looked out in the moonlight and observed water pouring around the breach on the eastern edge where the bank had collapsed.

"The next morning Mr. Hamlin came up with his team and he said the dam had moved, and he swung his horses around and ran them downtown and gave the alarm," Davis recalled. "He didn't stay there a second."

The "times likely to arise," referenced by T. Chalkley Hatton, had come. Because water overflowed the spillway, the 36-inch draw-off pipe through the center of the base of the dam was impossible to open. Its wooden cap was attached to the bell of the cast-iron pipe with wrought-iron clamps, under the water that rushed over the spillway.

Hatton arrived from his Delaware home to survey the situation and declared that something had to be done, and quickly, to relieve the pressure. He returned to Wilmington to prepare a recommendation. In the interim, out of desperation emerged a radical plan to blast out a section of the top of the dam, allowing enough water to escape so that the draw-off pipe could be opened to drain the rest of the reservoir. The engineers chose a section of concrete near the western hillside, opposite the landslide area from a few days earlier, and laced it with dynamite. As curious spectators looked on from a safe distance, a loud boom echoed down valley, audible even in Austin. Concrete shot out from the blast site. It plummeted to the valley floor on the south side and plunged into the water to the north. Instantly the water gushed through the gaping, jagged hole measuring about seven feet wide and extending downward to a point approximately four feet below the water's crest.

A corresponding breach was blasted on the eastern side.

## 1911 *The Austin Flood*

Freeman Run swelled with a swift, foamy current that advanced over the creek's banks, rushing down the valley. The lake's level was soon lowered to a point where the drainpipe could be accessed. The next obstacle was the thick wooden cap. Its removal was assigned to David Clark, "as daring a man as lives" (*Potter Enterprise*), who called for volunteers to assist. A dozen Austin men responded.

Clark worked himself out on the narrow breast of the dam to a point just above the outlet. Three times he lowered a satchel of sand containing several pounds of dynamite onto the pipe and detonated it with an electrical charge to blow off the plug. On each occasion, it failed. A fourth time he tried it with a bigger charge and the cap flew off and tumbled into the valley. Water shot out from the base of the pipe and rushed down the valley. "Whistles, bells and people all acclaimed joy and happiness," the *Enterprise* reported.

Disaster had been averted. By the following morning, almost half of the lake was gone, leaving puddles and a muddy mess in its upper stretches and a 20-foot-deep pool flush against the dam. The earthen dam that had been submerged upstream re-emerged, holding back a lake in the upper valley.

Theories abounded on what had caused the dam to slide and crack. Bayless and his advisors said publicly that they suspected the concrete had not been allowed to fully dry and harden after each successive layer was set. Most people knew better. The *Potter County Journal* reported in its February 2, 1910, edition, "A body of water 50 feet deep will exert a tremendous pressure against a perpendicular surface and this force moved the whole structure, foundation and all, with the middle springing the most. The foundation did not go deep enough to fasten into solid rock and hold the structure."

Newspaper articles in several cities grossly exaggerated the town's reaction to the leaking dam, telling of residents camped out in the mountains, freezing and starving because they were too frightened to return to their homes.

William Nelson called for a state investigation to assure that the structure was safe before the water level was permitted to rise again. Surprisingly, his voice was joined by John E. Baldwin, father of Bayless's lawyer. By that time, the younger Baldwin had parlayed his political connections to a seat in the Pennsylvania Senate. Their demands fell on deaf ears. The attitude of most Austin residents was best summarized by Olive McKinney. "At first we were scared. But after they emptied the dam, we all went back home, chased chickens out of the kitchen, washed the dishes and took up life where we left it. We just wanted a chance to work and live in peace. We were afraid Bayless might shut down and move the mill."

Bayless had no such intentions. Business was booming and company executives were working out refinancing options to expand their mills in Austin and Canada. Bayless now agreed that the valve and gate assembly that Hatton had so strongly recommended needed to be installed. Hamlin was directed to order the supplies.

Hatton was deeply troubled by the dam's compromised condition. He traveled to New York City to confer with Edward Wegmann Jr., formerly chief engineer of the New York Aqueduct Commission and a recognized expert on dam construction. The men agreed that the bow which pushed out from the dam's rim and its base was the result of upward pressure being exerted as water percolated through the sandstone and passed under the dam. Water had evidently softened a stratum of clay or shale lying between two layers of rock and permitted one of the layers to slip forward.

# 1911 *The Austin Flood*

**Hatton, February 8**: *My associate consulting engineer
[Wegmann] seemed to think that the cheapest thing to do
would be to reinforce the dam as it now stands, and that
this reinforcement would not be necessarily expensive. I
quite agree with him and feel that we should utilize the
dam that we have built up to its full capacity, which I feel
can be done at a great deal less cost than either doing
anything with the old dam or building a new one farther
up the stream.*

After studying the blueprints. Wegmann concluded that the
foundation was "extremely bad – porous sandstone, underlain
by strata of shale, with occasional seams of clay and gravel."
Together, the men developed two measures for reinforcing the
structure.

The first called for nearly doubling the cross-section of the
dam with concrete and increasing its weight by piling large
rocks and rubble as reinforcement against the southern
(downstream) face. This massive slope of heavy fill would
extend at about a 45-degree angle from the valley floor to a
point 10 feet from the dam's rim. A small dam, three or four
feet high, would be built to capture the water leaking through
the larger concrete structure and divert it to the mill. Cost was
estimated at $27,000.

A second element of the plan called for the excavation of a
large, concrete-filled ditch on the upstream side, excavated
down about nine feet to the impervious rock stratum – similar
to the cut-off wall Hatton had recommended earlier. This would
slightly lower the pressure on the dam and, most importantly,
would prevent water from traveling between the subterranean
layers and causing additional slippage of the foundation.
Estimated price tag for option two was $21,500.

Implicit in the men's recommendation was that the dam should remain empty unless both reinforcement measures were taken.

**Hatton, February 17**: *If Plan No. 2 is carried out, the dam would be entirely safe to carry water and all leakage would be prevented. I have also considered carrying the water in the dam at a lower elevation, but even if this was done the same cutoff wall would have to be built. We found by observation that the leaks under the dam existed as long as there was any water in the dam. If it was not for the cracks in the present dam, the concrete toe and conterforts would not have to be built, if the upper cutoff wall was made tight throughout. But these cracks have overcome the tension in the concrete and thus made it sectional instead of monolith, and I therefore would not care to insure its safety, except by reinforcement as shown in Plan No. 2. I appreciate the fact that the cost of repairing this dam appears very great but in light of our experience I feel neither of us would care to go through with what we have on account of this dam for double its cost, and I feel you will agree with me when I state that no makeshift device should be resorted to.*

Bayless had no intention of implementing any of his engineers' plan. He had quietly contacted another dam-builder, G. M. Miller from Kane, Pennsylvania, a town about 50 miles northwest of Austin. A day of reckoning was approaching.

**Bayless, February 21**: *It seems to us that the cost of the work is going to be practically as much as a new dam. I am enclosing a blueprint of another plan for reinforcing* *the dam. It is proposed to put up a timber dam behind the concrete wall with tie timbers eight feet on centers and all the crib work filled in with stone and dirt. There is a cutoff wall provided at the bottom of the slope, the intention being to put the cutoff wall down into the solid rock, but of course it is not nearly so wide a cutoff proposition as shown by your plan. It is further proposed to slush with concrete the front side of the filling next to the present masonry dam, and to bring the concrete covering down over the plank of the apron halfway, then to cover the balance of the apron and the slope behind the cutoff wall with clay. In addition to the above, we thought it might be advisable to excavate on the downstream side of the present masonry about five feet, below bottom of the present masonry two or three feet and put in two rows of one and one-half inch rods, drilling down into the bedrock and bringing them about to the present ground line. It looks to me as if this would give us fully as strong a dam as the repairs you propose and would not cost one-half as much. We will be glad to have your view in the matter.*

Hatton didn't mince his words in responding.

**Hatton, March 1.** *From an examination of the print I would surmise that the party who made the plan was not familiar with the topography of the valley. It would be quite impossible, and in fact impractical, to get such a bank water-tight with the material at hand, and the concrete cut-off wall would be useless. You propose making the joint between the present dam and the proposed filling water-tight by slushing in concrete and* *bringing this concrete covering down upon the apron about halfway. I believe this you would find impossible, as the concrete slushed in would be on a new filling which would be bound to settle and allow the water to get back of the concrete dam. In filling up between the timbers with stone and earth, great care would have to be taken to get this practically water-tight, and I know of no way of absolutely insuring this under such conditions and with such materials. I assume that you know that if the water gets under the present concrete dam, no matter from what source, it will cause this dam to slide upon its base no matter how much timber you may have against it on the upstream face. We have already proven without a doubt that a shallow cutoff wall will not prevent the water from getting under the concrete dam. If the water gets under the dam it will shove out. We have already proven that the character of the earth in the vicinity of the dam cannot be made water-tight. The one and one-half inch rods which you suggest putting down in the toe at the downstream face of the concrete dam would be of little avail in preventing slipping. The tendency against sliding can only be overcome by adding weight to the downstream face of the present dam, or by cutting off all possible leakage under the dam. No weight added to the upstream face would help the matter. It is my firm belief that it would be quite dangerous for you to adopt the timber reinforcement plan and would again jeopardize life and property below the dam.*

Bayless defended the plan, pointing out that Miller had solid references and "has had a large experience in building dams and has probably erected more than a hundred."

**Bayless, March 2**: *He guarantees to make the cutoff at the bottom of the slope entirely tight against leaking and to enter into a contract with us to complete this work within the next two months and at a figure about one-half what your estimate of this work is. We are inclined to give this plan careful consideration. The plans you submit will mean that we will be without the use of the dam all summer long and the cost is an unknown quantity, but I am inclined to think that we might better build a new dam than undertake to repair the old one on the plans you submit, so far as cost is concerned.*

Hatton tried one more time to warn Bayless.

**Hatton, March 3**: *I am still of the opinion that Mr. Miller will be unable to get his work water-tight with the cutoff wall proposed. We have already tried that with a far thicker and deeper wall and failed, and if it does get under his cutoff wall and through into his cribbing the full pressure will come upon the concrete dam which will either cause it to slide downstream further or leak out downstream so fast as to make you lose most of your water.*

Bayless shared his engineer's concerns with Miller, who convinced him that the log structure would take enough pressure off the concrete dam to prevent further slippage or cracking. Bayless pointed out that the lake had recently reached a depth of 36 feet and the dam had not budged.

**Bayless, March 8**: *Inasmuch as the dam is sufficiently strong to hold the pressure of the water, a cutoff wall three or four feet thick and going to impervious strata would* *seem to be just as good as a heavier wall, especially if waterproof material is used in its construction. If, after doing the work as outlined, it should be found that there were still leaks in the structure, it would then be possible without interfering with the operation of the dam to add a further reinforcement wall along the front of the dam as shown by your Plan No. 2. Therefore, it seems to me it would be as well to adopt the cheaper plan on the start and in case any leak shows, to further strengthen it in accordance with Plan No. 2, as above stated, because we have practically proved that the dam has found a secure footing and will not slide further. We have 36 feet of water behind the concrete dam and are digging a trench in front of the dam so as to collect all the leakage and this we are turning into the main pipe line to the mill which we have opened. Besides the leakage, we are using a little extra water from the concrete dam. Meanwhile, we are going to put in a wooden dam between the ice house and the first house below the road. We expect to have this in by the first of June and until then we will be able to run with the water now holding behind the broken dam. If we can fill up the wooden dam, it will carry us through the summer in good shape and with the same we will be able either this fall or early next spring to repair the present structure. Otherwise, if we started to make repairs on the dam at this time, we would be without water another season which we cannot afford.*

Miller said he could build the log dam for $11,000 and have it in place by June 1. It would be sloped to reduce pressure, thickest in the middle and tapered toward either bank, much like an arrow tip pointing upstream. The theory was that the heavy force of the 150 million gallons of water behind it would wedge it tighter, similar to a beaver dam.

As soon as the frost had left the ground, Miller's crew began excavating. It was a relatively simple structure, the eight-foot-long timbers tied together and cribbing filled with stones and dirt.

Members of the Association of Engineering Societies inspected the site after the lake was lowered. Their findings were published in the March 17, 1910, edition of *Engineering News*, bluntly warning that the concrete dam, if it were allowed to be filled again, could fail. "Nothing has been done toward reinforcing this structure," they declared.

Bayless had other battles to fight. Equipment malfunctions interrupted production and a flood of Canadian paper imports threatened his domestic manufacturers. He was also having difficulty recruiting and retaining skilled workers. "The trouble is we have been letting the good men get away and working in Italians to an extent where they are so numerous and make so many mistakes they are more nuisance than they are worth," Fred Hamlin lamented in a letter to his boss. "It makes a long payroll and we do not get the work done as well as it should be. I wish we could get hold of some good men and let some of the poor riff raff go."

Workers patched the cracks in the concrete structure and repaired the breach that had been blasted from the eastern rim. They also installed the long overdue valve and wooden gate system. The moon-shaped dynamited section on the western end was partially built up with concrete. Once the patches had dried, Bayless's men concluded that the dam was strong enough to hold more water.

Austin's vibrant Main Street (looking west) in late 19th century prior to fires and floods.

Flood waters that struck in 1889 were one of several challenges the expanding community of Austin was able to meet and defeat. Photo at right shows western hillside south of town, not yet stripped of its virgin timber.

**Devastating 1890 fire leveled Austin's business district.**

**Lumbering industry fueled the region's economic boom.**

Goodyear Lumber Company dominated Austin. B&S Railroad depot is shown at left.

## From Hills to Mills

Cut and skidded from the hillsides and carried by Goodyear's pioneering railroads, logs were processed into millions of board feet of lumber.

**Stacks of finished lumber fill the Freeman Run valley.**

**It was long hours and hard work for laborers at the hardwood mill.**

**Costello's tannery was the world's biggest.**

**Goodyear pond and view of mill looking north.**

**Massive kindling works of Standard Wood Company.**

## Impressive Austin

Austin was the envy of northern Pennsylvania after rebuilding in brick from early floods and fires. Facing west in the upper photos and east below.

Goodyear's B&S depot was the community hub.

New department store just a few steps from the depot.

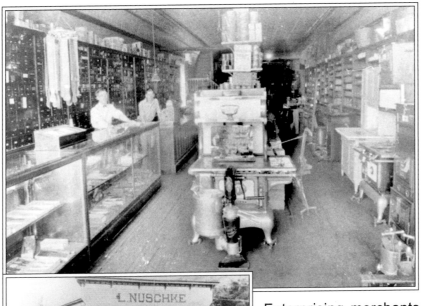

Enterprising merchants like the Nuschkes and Moores set up shop in Austin to provide a lively and growing community with an expanded line of products and services.

## Growing Affluence

Austin's post office, bank, telephone switchboard and other offices shared this Main Street building. Turner Street (below) was one of the more well-to-do sections.

## Serving the Community

A hospital was established in the former Goodyear home on a terraced street by the same name overlooking the town. Methodist Episcopal (right) and Presbyterian churches and parsonages.

A large leather tannery brought rapid growth to Costello.

Railroad depot was Costello's link to the outside world.

# E. O. Austin, town founder

## *Pioneer of Freeman Run valley*

Edward O. and Julia Austin left their roots in Steuben County, N.Y., in 1856, and established a home at the junction of Freeman Run's two forks, the beginnings of a lively community that would later bear their name.

# Frank H. Goodyear

## *Goodyear Lumber Co.*

Austin was the base of operations for the extensive Goodyear empire. As resources were depleted, the Goodyears left the valley for Louisiana.

**Charles W. Goodyear**

# A.G. Lyman and his hardwood mill

### *Emporium Lumber Company*

Lyman cut the hardwood on Goodyear lands in his mill, two miles south of Austin. It ran from 1890 to 1901, when he sold it to the Emporium Lumber Company, which continued to purchase and cut Goodyear's hardwood.

**Logs fill the pond at the Goodyear mill**

## Frank E. Baldwin
### Senator, attorney

The influential Frank Baldwin (above and at far right in top photo) played a major role in bringing Bayless to Austin. His sister, Grace Baldwin Collins, tried in vain to rescue their parents.

## Michael Murrin
### Burgess

Murrin had the dubious honor of balancing loyalties to the town and to his employer, Bayless

## William Nelson
### *Austin's 'Jeremiah'*

More vocal than most to express fear of the dam, his warnings went unheeded. He and his wife died in the flood.

## Cora Brooks
### *Austin's Madam*

Many in Austin were warned of impending doom when Brooks, upon witnessing the dam begin to break up, telephoned in the first alarm to the town.

# George C. Bayless

*President, Bayless Pulp & Paper Company*

# T. Chalkley Hatton

*Chief Consulting Engineer*

## Heroines

Switchboard operator Kathleen Lyons held her post until the last minute. Operators Lena Binckey (lower right) and Hazel Knapp (lower left) also sounded the warning.

Telephone operator Lena Binckey gathers her thoughts.

Bell System telephone workers pitched in.

**Cornelius Buckley**

**Herb Young**

**Lena Binckey's mother counts her blessings.**

**Pennsylvania Governor John Tener (left)**
Traveled to Austin to pledge the state's support.

**Dr. Samuel G. Dixon**
*State Health
Commissioner*

**William H. Taft**
*U.S. President*

## State Constabulary

Uniformed officers kept order in the stricken community and assisted in rescue and recovery.

## Medical staff

Doctors and nurses from a wide-spread area rushed to the disaster scene and were put to work in many capacities, from rendering medical care to distributing food and comforting the bereaved.

Bayless mill converted piles of pulpwood to tons of paper and Austin's prospects from bleak to promising.

Upper, pulpwood awaits processing. Middle, a rare glimpse inside the Bayless mill. Lower, small earthen dam provided by the Borough of Austin.

**Construction of the Bayless dam began in 1909.**

As the concrete dam took shape, few were aware of its structural shortcomings.

Many were troubled in January 1910 when an early thaw filled the lake to capacity. Worse yet, a bow could be seen near the center of the structure, suggesting it was unable to hold back the weight exerted by hundreds of millions of gallons of water.

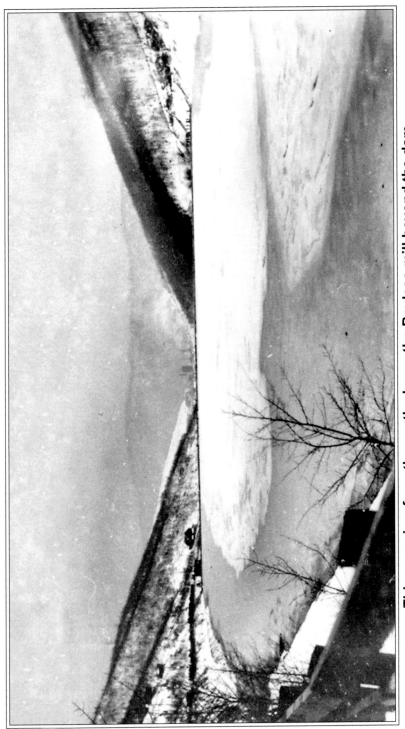

This rare view from the north shows the Bayless mill beyond the dam.

January 1910: The dam was clearly beginning to yield to the pressure, bowing at the brim and leaking underneath.

## Construction and Reinforcement Plans

General plan of dam project showing construction support facilities and inset of dam profile. In box is consulting engineer Wegmann's proposed reinforcement after Jan. 1910 scare. Arrows point to earth/rock fill wall and all-important cutoff wall. None of his recommendations were implemented.

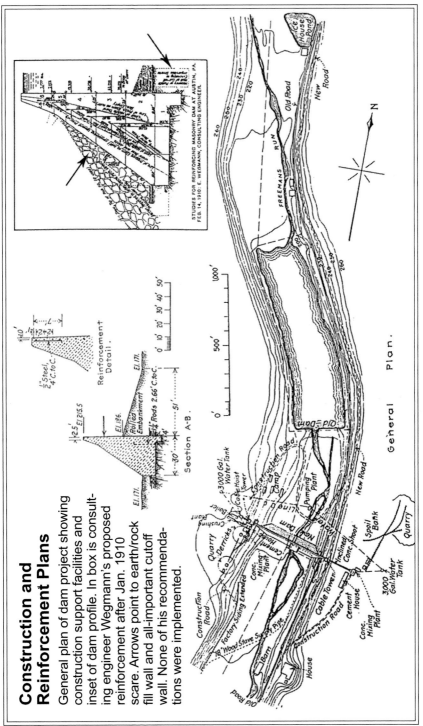

STUDIES FOR REINFORCING MASONRY DAM AT AUSTIN, PA.
FEB. 14, 1910: E. WEGMANN, CONSULTING ENGINEER.

Reinforcement Detail.

Section A-B.

General Plan.

# THE BAYLESS DAMS

Three dams were built across Freeman Run to supply water to the paper mill. Here's help in distinguishing one from another.

**Earthen dam:** Built in 1900 by the Austin Borough; swept away in the concrete dam failure, only the spillway remains today.

**Concrete dam:** Built in 1909 by C.J. Brintnall & Co., Binghamton, N.Y., T.C. Hatton, engineer; failed Sept. 30, 1911.

**Log crib dam:** Built in 1910 by G.M. Miller, Kane, Pa., after the January scare; later reinforced by earth banks; breached in the 1942 flood; still in existence, it is known by locals as the dirt dam.

# 6

## *Better Safe Than Sorry*

Warmer, drier weather created another water shortage at the paper mill. The drought continued until October, when a long period of rainy days swelled the lake behind the concrete dam to 35 feet. The log dam also filled, albeit with much less water than Miller had promised it could hold. It was evident that the contractor had cut corners. Blueprints called for it to be 32 feet high, but its actual height was 30 feet. Miller also skimped on rock fill along the downstream side and failed to tamp the soil in between each bent of the dam.

No one was more fearful of the concrete dam, or more vocal in his concerns, than William Nelson. He has been described in some historical accounts as the "Jeremiah of Austin," in reference to the Biblical figure whose prophecy of doom for the city of Jerusalem was belittled as blasphemy. Nelson regularly took his horse and wagon up Freeman Run to closely monitor the concrete dam, searching for signs of weakness. On one of his visits, he was aghast to discover a new stream flowing from under the structure.

Some Austin residents shared Nelson's concern. W. R. Miller, a railroad official who spent much of his time in Austin, told a reporter, "I never went to sleep in the hotel there without a mighty fervent prayer that the inevitable might be delayed. I always felt that we might be swept away in the night."

Under pressure, Bayless agreed to limit the water level of the lake to no more than 40 feet, in an effort to reduce pressure on the dam.

Austin was abuzz in mid-October 1910 after a well-known local laborer, Richard Ripple, was shot dead during a scuffle at madam Cora Brooks' brothel, overlooking the dam on the eastern hillside. Painting contractor Jesse D. Robinson, a self-described drifter and morphine addict, was convicted of second-degree murder and sentenced to 20 years in jail.

Brooks' establishment had caused quite a stir in the thriving community. It was referred to by its postal address, "Number 31," by those too uncomfortable to call it what it was. Women lowered their voices when they spoke of Cora and her ladies. The fact that her house was located so far from town was no coincidence. Not only could her customers come and go with less visibility, the business was also more tolerable to Austin's proper citizens—out of sight, out of mind.

"But the disreputable business that was the real cause of the awful tragedy still flourishes in the very heart of decent civilization," the *Potter Enterprise* editorialized after Robinson was sentenced. "Why should the strong arm of protection be thrown about this crime breeder? The inmates of this place come to town, in their silks and satins and fancy hats, and more than one child in Austin who needs clothes to make him respectable and comfortable must go without, while the father spends money in this vile place."

Hopes were raised for an economic boost across Potter

County due to the early returns of natural gas drilling. Townspeople anticipated that Austin's population, set at 2,941 in the 1910 census, would soon surpass the 3,000 milestone. Bell Telephone Company proudly proclaimed that it was extending service to many remote sections for customer groups as small as a half-dozen homes. Community leaders were assured that the Bayless plant would continue to prosper.

Behind the scenes, however, George Bayless knew his mill's water demands would never be fully met by Freeman Run and he fretted about the impractical combination of three dams that now extended up the valley in this letter to Hamlin:

**Bayless, December 2**: *Some of our directors are rather worried about the possibility of trouble with the upper (log) dam and think if it broke, a big flood of water would be let down against the lower dam and possibly cause serious trouble. Therefore, to avoid any possibility of trouble, or any criticism on account of lack of care on our part, I wish you would immediately, as directed by phone, blast out the spillway of the lower dam to 35 feet. This would probably satisfy our stockholders here as well as the people in Austin. I wish you would keep this office advised as to the conditions of the upper dam and whether same is leaking to any extent, and how much, and where; also, if the dam is getting soaked up and tighter, or whether the leaks are increasing.*

**Hamlin, December 3**: *As regards the wooden dam, it filled last night to within four feet, one inch of the overflow, but was leaking quite a little, and this morning when I went up about ten o'clock, I found that it had dropped about six inches. This may be from two causes, falling off from the flow of the creek on account of two cold days* *and nights and the leak that we have had, being the same, or the leak may be worse and in that case it has taken all the flow of the creek as well as six inches off the entire pond. There are leaks all along and in a number of places on the west side the water is coming out of the bank about one and one-half feet above the flat land along a seam of rocks. This leak started when the dam began to fill up. There is quite a leak on the east side right where the bank begins to raise from the bottom. It shows on the south side, but the dam seems to stand up level and straight. The only thing I can see is that it settled about 10 inches clear across the valley. This is possibly due to the timber settling together with the weight of the water.*

**Bayless, December 7**: *I hope that you will find that most of the leakage is around the gate due to the wicket not being tight, because we can easily overcome this trouble. However, as soon as the dam is emptied, have all the different leaks carefully marked, examined and made tight in so far as possible, and then we will again fill the dam. If it then holds comparatively tight, we will let the water out of the lower dam and put in the large three-foot gate, which we ought to have done in the first place.*

At this point, the library of correspondence at the Potter County Historical Society Museum ends.

The year 1911 dawned with Austin clearly established as the region's most progressive community. The long-awaited paving of Main Street was about to begin, as work crews began to grade the dirt roadbed. Their work was interrupted by persistent heavy rains that ruined much of what they had accomplished and created a muddy mess.

Work at the Goodyear hemlock mill was cut back to a single

shift and orders were sporadic. Some of the Goodyear equipment was dismantled and taken to another of the company's lumber mills in western Pennsylvania.

Following persistent public outcry, Brooks' establishment was finally raided and she was arrested for operating a "bawdy house" and selling liquor without a license.

William Nelson continued his evening routine. On one occasion, he and a friend passed by Superintendent Hamlin's house en route to the dam and stopped to talk.

"Seems to me you fellows are badly troubled about the dam," said Hamlin.

"All I've got is below it," Nelson retorted.

"Do you think that we would have built the mills below it if it weren't safe? You had better quit disturbing people's minds, or it will hurt your business," Hamlin replied.

The superintendent's actions spoke louder than his words. He had built his own house on what was known as Bayless Row, a short distance below the mill on a hillside. Hamlin's wife told a newspaper reporter that her husband had his own reservations. "I kept telling Mr. Hamlin that I wanted to move down to Turner Street, which was the place where the best families of Austin lived," she said. "He said he preferred to stay on the hill. I asked him whether he was afraid of the dam and he said, 'I'm not exactly afraid of the dam, but you can never tell. I want my family to be on the safe side of the hill if it ever does break'."

A late August news story from the little town of Ketner, about 30 miles south of Austin, caused some unrest. A new concrete dam built to serve a chemical company gave way. Many homes and businesses were destroyed.

Hearing that, Emporium Lumber Company manager Everritt Van Wert decided to ship the mill's more valuable products out of town. "We felt the danger was serious enough to warrant a thinning out of our highest grade of hardwoods," Van Wert explained. "I talked to George Bayless about the dam and he assured me that the new work and the new reinforcement put in had made the structure absolutely safe. He told me he had the best engineering advice on it and was perfectly satisfied that it would never make trouble again." A few Austin business operators followed Emporium Lumber Company's lead and moved their more valuable merchandise out of the valley.

Heavy rains that fell over the September 15-17 weekend caused the lake behind the concrete dam to rise within inches of the brim. An even larger volume of leakage gushed forth from underneath the structure. The added pressure was also evident upstream at the timber dam, where Bayless workers were dispatched to add more soil, timber and stone reinforcement.

Those scattered trees that survived the lumbermen's saws began to preview their glorious fall foliage. In the September 28 edition of the *Austin Autograph*, readers were informed that some of the heaviest rainfall on record had been recorded over the past several weeks. Another story told of the upcoming Buffalo and Susquehanna Railroad family picnic. Scarlet fever, typhoid and "consumption" were identified as persistent health menaces and North Pennsylvania General Hospital was recruiting more students for nursing classes.

Austin United Methodist Church proudly proclaimed that 181 people attended the most recent Sunday School classes. Too many "mere boys" were said to be smoking cigarettes in Austin. Community leaders reported that a deal to relocate a knitting mill to Austin was imminent; the company's owners were tired of the higher taxes and overhead at their Philadelphia location.

The *Autograph* also reminded citizens of their duty to vote in Saturday's election. Readers were encouraged to board the railroad and ride out to Watrous in eastern Potter County to check out the new oil wells, another sure sign of prosperity for the region.

And evangelist Billy Sunday warned that "the world is going to Hell so fast that it's breaking the speed limit."

**1911**  *The Austin Flood*

# 7

## *Head For The Hills!*

Saturday, September 30, dawned bright and sunny in Austin, a typical Indian summer day. The town was buzzing with Election Day activity. Voters were drawn in particular to the race for the three seats on the Potter County Board of Commissioners, and townspeople were anxious to show their support for their hometown favorite, Republican Charles D. Austin, son of the town's founder. Women's suffrage was yet to come, so the polls at Town Hall were largely populated by men. Saturday was also a busy shopping day, both for the locals and for travelers lodged at the Commercial Hotel and the Goodyear Hotel. Women were buying their week's supplies of groceries.

Shortly after daybreak, Oscar Clafflin hitched a horse to his wagon and rode up to the dam, passing over property he sold Austin Borough more than a decade earlier to help bring the Bayless mill to town. He was one of the laborers hired to stabilize the log dam and was on his way to work.

"The water was just below the spillway, about a half-inch

from flowing over," Clafflin said. "When there would come a wind, it would go right over the spillway in a riffle. It had breaks in the dam where it first gave—and the water was squirting out of them, instead of running out them pail-like as it had. It was squirting 20 feet right in the air from that dam."

Walking around to the east side, Clafflin spotted Michael Bailey, the man assigned by George Bayless to monitor the lake's water level and operate the discharge gate. "I says to Mr. Bailey, 'What in the name of God are you keeping so much water for?' And he says, 'You have a big head like lots of those downtown.' Then I says, 'Mr. Bailey you know that dam is liable to go any time. Why don't you let the gate open and let the water down? What the hell's the use of holding water like that?' And I went on with my work."

Bailey did go to the paper mill to inform Hamlin that the water was running over the spillway. The superintendent instructed him keep the gate closed, since George Bayless wanted to dam to be as full as possible to meet production demands at the plant. Water from the week's heavy rains was pouring into the valley so fast that it would have overflowed the dam anyhow, even if the gate had been opened.

Hamlin also fielded a telephone call that morning from Bob Pearson, one of his employees. Pearson relayed the conversation to a newspaper reporter:

"I went up to the dam in the morning and I saw some cracks. The water was coming up rapidly. I knew it was not safe. I rushed to the telephone at the roadhouse and called up Mr. Hamlin. I said, 'Mr. Hamlin, I think the dam's gonna break— what should we do?' He answered, 'I don't think we need to worry.' I urged him to let some water out and he said, 'Don't cry until you are hurt.' Hamlin didn't think of my wife and my little children. He didn't think of Austin. All he could think of was saving up a little water against a dry spell. God, he's crying now after he's hurt."

At his grocery store, William Nelson was fuming to any customer who would listen. "I went up to Austin to get some groceries at Nelson's Store," recalled John Brownlee from Costello. "When I got there, Will was mad. Said he and Bob Pearson wanted them to let water out of the dam, but Hamlin got angry and called them a bunch of big heads. He said they didn't know what they were talking about and shouldn't be stirring up trouble. He told Will people ought to be happy to have a job."

Horses with wagons or buggies were hitched to posts on Main Street. Politicians and their supporters were working the streets. About a half-dozen woodhicks waited their turn for a haircut and a shave at Grisbow's Barber Shop. On the hillside, dozens of townspeople crowded into a school classroom for a children's theatrical performance.

Suddenly a fire whistle split the morning air. Curious townspeople stepped outside to see what the commotion was about. It was a false alarm, accidentally triggered by workmen repairing telephone lines. A half-hour or so later, the siren sounded once more, set off again by the linemen.

At the Bayless mill, a partial crew was busy unloading freshly cut pulpwood hauled in by rail, adding it to the mountainous stacks already awaiting processing. The swollen lake behind the Bayless dam lapped at the concrete wall. The water's choppy surface reflected the blue hue from above and puffy white clouds that dotted the sky like cotton balls.

———

Harry Davis was enjoying a peaceful afternoon at the house where he had been boarding with Cora Brooks. Davis was the unofficial sentinel designated to keep check of the dam. Around 2 o'clock, as he nodded off to sleep, he was jarred by a rumble in the ground and an ominous sound of cracking and heaving in the valley below. A huge section, almost round and eight to ten feet in diameter, shot out from four or five feet above the dam's base, west of the center.

Water roared through the gap. Seconds later, a large piece above the opening broke away and rolled into the valley below. The walls above and around it tumbled as water gushed relentlessly forward. East of the spillway, a tall column of the dam slid southward at a slight angle. Another pivoted like a hinged gate at an angle of about 45 degrees.

Breaches appeared everywhere as the structure, now compromised, helplessly surrendered to the water's force. The gaps widened, and water swung in a massive wave, spilling over the flattened sections and reducing the pressure on the tall, thick columns. They seemed to be holding their ground, but eventually yielded, like the immense gates of a canal lock.

John Newman, a politician from Coudersport, was driving past the dam with a friend. Newman shared his observations:

"I said, 'It seems to me that there's an awful lot of water coming over it today,' and then a big lump popped out of place and catapulted down the stream. I shouted, 'By God, there it goes!' Then, like the cracking of a whip, another part snapped out. In what seemed like another second, the great mass of wood pulp down the valley was being flicked into the air like matches. It went up like a cloud. The smokestacks of the Bayless mill were hidden behind the spray and the cracking logs."

Fred Keck and L. B. Seibert from Coudersport also witnessed the shocking spectacle while driving north on the narrow roadway along the east side. They looked on in shock as the gushing water zeroed in on the home of an elderly couple, Adam and Jennie Broadt. Mrs. Broadt, sitting on the porch, rose and peered toward the roadway south of the dam where her husband was driving his horse. Keck and Seibert watched helplessly as the flood first engulfed Adam Broadt and seconds later swept up his wife and the home.

By that time, Davis had raced inside, yelling to Brooks and anyone else who was within earshot. He grabbed the telephone to alert the Bayless mill. His call was answered by Margaret Decker, who at first thought he was kidding. When she realized he was serious, it was too late. Instead of sounding the warning whistle, Decker and other office staffers fled for their lives, shouting to others as they ran. It was only later, after the flood had passed, that someone triggered the mill's alarm

Davis went back outside while Brooks phoned in to warn the town of Austin. Her call was fielded at the central switchboard on the second floor of the bank building by Lena Binckey, one of three Bell Telephone System operators on duty at the time. Binckey, Kathleen V. Lyons and Hazel Knapp instantly sprung into action.

Due to doubts about the dam, there was an understanding that a continual whistle from the Standard Kindling Wood Works was the signal that the dam had given way. Women and children in particular had been coached to run if they heard the alarm. But Binckey's call was misunderstood at the mill. As a result, the desk man at the plant sounded the usual alarm to warn of a fire—eight short toots and then a sustained whistle.

Operator Lyons, who was just 16 years old, also called the Goodyear mill, instructing an office clerk to trigger the alarm. While Binckey and Knapp set out on foot to sound the warning, Lyons remained at the switchboard to call as many subscribers as she could, both in town and at Costello, three miles down the valley.

The initial surge reached the immense piles of pulpwood stacked in the mill yard, immediately north of the Bayless plant. Most of the 700,000 cords of 50-inch stacked wood and portions of the immense timber stock were lifted by the current and thrust forward, riding the crest like battering rams into portions of the mill's four buildings.

A handful of Bayless employees heard the deep, low roar and knew what it meant. Others who worked in the lower departments, mostly young women hired to count paper, could not hear the shouted warnings or the advancing waters because of the noise of machinery. Messengers from the office warned most of the other departments in time for employees to flee to the western hillside before the flood's fury burst upon the buildings.

Large sections of the mill on the western side escaped serious damage, thanks to the valley's eastward slope. On the eastern flat, however, walls collapsed and machinery was smashed. M. A. Devereaux, caught in the grinding room, grasped the shafting above him as the wall caved in. Eventually, he lost his grip and fell helplessly into the torrent. When he resurfaced, he was swept into the tangled machinery, legs-first, and lodged there as the waters rushed over him. Devereaux screamed for help until he was pulled from the wreckage two hours later with both legs broken.

Emery Worth, working in the plant's second-story tying room, said water was hissing as it shot through the broken dam. "Thinking a steam pipe had blown up, I looked up from my work just in time to see the room cave in," he said. "I was thrown out of the window and onto the roof, which landed me high and dry."

Employee Arthur Brown watched developments unfold

from the roof. "I first saw a large pile of wood and then a big body of water sort of crowning over on top of it like an ocean wave. The big wave seemed like it was gaining on the wood pile. I was worried for my wife. I hadn't seen her since about seven o'clock that morning."

It turned out that Anna Brown, 33, had walked downtown about 10 minutes before the flood hit and made a desperate but unsuccessful run for her life. Her battered body was found near the ruins of the Catholic Church at the foot of the western hillside.

Five lives were lost at the mill. Eleven employees were injured. The water was moving so quickly that some of the mill workers survived by holding their breath while submerged.

Roaring, crashing, twisting and picking up everything in its path, the wave surged forward. Three young children playing in a sand pile next to the mill were swept to their deaths. Oscar Clafflin's two houses succumbed to an overlapping upper crest 25 feet high that sucked them into the maelstrom along with all of his possessions.

The earthen dam upstream fell victim to physics and gravity. As the forewall was sucked away by the vacuum effect of the surge, pressure from water upstream crumbled the structure, providing even more force to the current.

A warning whistle from the Goodyear Mill and the town's fire alarm wailed in dissonance through the valley. Tragically, many Austin residents thought nothing of it, having been irritated already by the telephone linemen's false alarms.

Roughly 15 minutes would elapse between the dam's failure and the flood's arrival in Austin. Reactions varied, from those who immediately fled, to others who stopped to gather valuables and paid the ultimate price. Many refused to join the mass exodus, believing the flood waters would, at worst, be a messy nuisance. Still others stayed in the valley to help others. Volunteer firefighters yanked the single-hose cart onto Main Street and whirled around the corner to Railroad Avenue, looking for smoke, before they realized this emergency was no fire. Movie theater operator and carpenter John J. Deziel, standing on the hillside with his sister, shouted to the firemen. They dropped their ropes and climbed up in time.

Four schoolgirls walking arm-in-arm along Main Street and looking for smoke in the sky were not so fortunate. After helping the firemen to safety, Deziel's sister screamed for the girls to run, but they couldn't hear her and their fate was sealed.

The torrent carrying hundreds of logs and parts of the paper mill rocked and ricocheted down the valley "like a huge slithering snake," one witness recounted, moving up one hillside and sliding down another, gathering houses in the process. A quiet rumble that could be heard faintly in Austin grew to a loud roar and the ground shook as a rising mist moved closer to the town. Witnesses on surrounding hillsides could see little or no water, but rolling debris foretold catastrophe. People seemed bewildered as to which way to turn for escape. Some remained in their tracks, transfixed.

Boyd Lockhard, a young businessman, casually stepped outside, assuming another false alarm, and looked up the valley. He scrambled to safety in the nick of time. "It looked like a wall of wood, 25 feet high," Lockhard told a reporter. "At first glance I did not see the water at all, because the wood from the pulp mill was carried before it, tearing away at buildings. I ran towards the hill and got above the level of water while it was surging within 10 feet of me. The ground began to give way under me but I managed to climb a few feet higher and caught hold of a tree."

Residents of Rukgaber Street, running parallel to Freeman

Run at the foot of the eastern hillside, had only a short distance to climb. The situation was similar on Turner Street, the corresponding road at the foot of the western hillside, with one critical difference. Those fleeing the flood waters there ran into a series of high, barbed-wire fences erected to keep grazing cows from wandering into town.

Some ran south toward Main Street, where they could veer to the right and without having to contend with fences. A number of people positioned themselves next to the barbed wire fence and helped others to reach safety, in some instances at their own peril. Residents of Railroad Street had to decide whether to wade across the swelling Freeman Run or run south to Main Street and then try to make it up either hillside.

Homes on Rukgaber, Turner and Railroad streets took the full brunt of the attack, adding their wreckage to the wave that cascaded southward. Houses that were not shattered were shoved sideways into the hillside. The last structure north of Main Street to yield was Austin's majestic Presbyterian Church, which heaved and rocked before being ripped from its foundation, largely intact. The church, complete with its signature arched beams above the sanctuary, would ride the crest of the tide for more than two miles, finally collapsing in the picnic grove near Costello.

Bell System operator Kathleen Lyons took the dislodging of the church as her cue to abandon the switchboard. The telephone office was upstairs in the combined post office and bank building on the western end of Main Street, so she didn't have far to travel. By the time she reached the hillside, water lapped at her heels.

At least a dozen people owed their lives to another hero, described in newspaper accounts only as "a hatless man," who dashed into the election polls at Town Hall shouting that the dam had burst.

A bridge across Freeman Run on Main Street was a lifesaver for many. Tailor Frank McLaughlin told of crossing the bridge and reaching safety, only to look back and see a dozen or more men or women who followed be washed away.

Where there once were tree-shaded streets, not a sign of vegetation remained. The Catholic church, while not in the center of the path of the flood, was lifted and hurled into a broken mass against the hillside. Its steeple cross was directed at right angles to the foot of the mountain.

The brick buildings of Main Street's northern side offered stiff resistance, fueling a false hope that they might hold back the mighty torrent. However, most of them collapsed as logs and debris smashed into the structures. The four-story brick hotel was razed as clean as if a wrecking crew had taken it away. The three-story opera house was shattered into kindling.

Another row of brick structures, lining the southern side of Main Street, fared somewhat better. The second floor took the brunt of the attack, in some cases causing the third story to fall and flatten the first floor. Against the buildings that held their ground grew a mountain of timber, smashed houses, bricks and household items while the wave moved on.

From the safety of the hillsides, some survivors covered their eyes and ears as they heard the shrieks of victims amid the loud roar. A few knelt and prayed. Two of the eyewitnesses would hysterically share their observations with reporter Louis F. Kirby of *The North American*:

"They said that, on the roof of one of the houses, as it passed them on the hillside, six little children were huddled, clinging to one another for protection. As the house was whirled along, another floating building struck it broadside. The children, shaken from their insecure footing, were hurled from the roof and swallowed in the flood."

Wreckage that piled where the valley takes a sharp turn beyond Main Street was compressed to a height of about 75 feet. Austin was piped for natural gas and the great force of the water tore the mains from the streets. Something sparked the gas that was pouring out of the mangled pipes to ignite. There was no explosion, but the huge pile of driftwood erupted in flames. Within minutes, other gas pipes were pouring their fuel into the air. Flames, blown by a strong wind, spread from house to house until they hit a barren stretch.

Town Hall was lifted from its foundation, walls collapsing as its second story sunk. Fortunately, there were no prisoners in the steel cells of the basement.

Austin's bank and post office, owned by the Baylesses and Senator Baldwin, took a hit but held its ground. The flood swept away much of the furniture and other contents of the upstairs telephone office and a doctor's examining room.

Among the hardest-hit properties were the once-thriving shops of the Buffalo and Susquehanna Railroad and the lumber mills. Half of the large Goodyear plant, including a 40-foot-tall brick kiln and dozens of chimneys, were reduced to rubble and its smaller buildings swept away. An alert employee of the Goodyear mill had rushed to the engine room and tied down the fire alarm, assuring that its loud, deep-toned whistle sounded without interruption. As that section of the mill broke off, it floated on the current, the whistle blaring ominously as it was carried more than a mile before it collapsed.

Crushed homes, lumber and other items carried by the flood piled against the Buffalo & Susquehanna Railroad shops and ignited. Broken gas pumps fueled the fire. At least three of the railroad's employees perished.

Goodyear's log pond was filled to overflowing with

wreckage. Among its contents was a train car load of paper weighing more than 10 tons that floated down from the Bayless mill. Standard Lumber Company had recently prepared a large stock of stove wood for shipment. As burning gas broke through the building, it ignited this potent fuel, creating a massive bonfire that would last long into the night.

Workers on the B&S train, which was stopped on the main line south of Main Street, leapt from the boxcars and ran to the eastern hillside just before the flood waters picked up the long train and dragged it away. Several of its cars and parts of the B&S passenger station ended up in the millpond of the Emporium Lumber Company, almost a mile downstream. Other cars, loaded with coal and weighing hundreds of tons, came to rest about 200 yards south of the track. Two of them stood upended, forming an inverted "V" which collected at its apex a thick pile of hay and other debris. The B&S tracks became a twisted, distorted mass of iron south of the village.

As the valley grew wider, it slowed the flood's pace and allowed debris to spread out along the water's surface. J. C. Borchard, who lived just north of Costello, watched a sea of water, logs, shattered buildings and bricks sweep past him in the valley below. He reported that the initial surge was covered with newly sawn timber and pieces of lumber. Five or six minutes elapsed before pieces of housetops, broken furniture and other remnants of Austin's destruction could be seen.

Brothers Herb and Edward Young were working at the Emporium Lumber Company when word of the disaster arrived. Hatless and coatless, they hopped on their bicycles and headed south. Herb Young stopped at the Brownlee flour mill, about one mile north of Costello, to sound the warning. Owner William Brownlee and three employees reached the hillside just in time to see the mill swept away.

Hearing the roar behind them, the Young brothers pedaled even faster. Herb stopped at his own house to warn his wife and help his son, Matthew, climb onto the handlebars. They rode through the village shouting a warning to everyone within earshot.

Switchboard operator Kathleen Lyons had only reached a handful of phone customers in Costello before she fled her post. Costello was also warned by George Peek, an insurance agent from Olean, New York. He was visiting relatives in Costello and had started for Austin in a car with a chauffeur and four children. In the distance, Peek spotted the approaching flood. The driver reversed direction on the narrow highway and sped back to Costello. The car came cruising down Main Street, its horn blaring and all six of its occupants shouting out the windows.

Moments later, a rising mist could be seen to the north, followed by a dull rumble that grew more ominous as each second passed. A bridge across the junction of a small tributary and Freeman Run was ripped from its foundation and swept up in the debris riding the gushing tide. Soon, a massive wall of logs and lumber, trees and partial houses, human carnage and everything that bowed to the water's fury swept through Costello. A section of wooden buildings in the village's center crumbled. Others were pulled from their foundations intact. Brick structures fared better.

Water and debris snaked its way around the sprawling tannery, which was just far enough up the slope to survive the onslaught. The railroad bridge nearby was lifted and carried about 500 feet before lodging on the pitched bank south of town. Because the town had ample warning, just two of Costello's residents died.

A steep mountainside on Costello's southeast side redirected the weakening surge southwestward where it spread out over the wider valley toward the village of Wharton. By the time the flow reached the town of Sinnemahoning at the mouth of the First Fork in the early evening, the lake north of Austin was gone and Freeman Run had returned to its normal flow, albeit in newly created crevices. Some lumber survived the voyage more than 50 miles, all the way into the Susquehanna River.

# 8

## *Life Or Death*

Split-second decisions made the difference between life and death. Most of the fatalities were the result of the victims being battered or crushed, rather than drowning. There were miraculous escapes, incredible rescues, and tragic losses as one loved one was torn from another. Amid the horror came stories of courage and triumph.

Lafayette "Lafe" Starkweather, a Civil War veteran and prosperous real estate broker, had just left his second floor apartment in one of the brick buildings on Main Street when he was warned. He hurried back to alert his wife, Harriett, who assured him she would be right behind him. As Starkweather neared Nuschke's Furniture Store near the foot of the hill, he was alarmed to discover that Harriett was nowhere in sight. He ran back to the apartment, where he found her frantically gathering possessions. With the roar of the flood within earshot, Starkweather pleaded with his wife to join him. Off he dashed again, reaching the front of Nuschke's at the same time the flood waters smashed into the back of the store.

As a portion of the building collapsed, a large plate glass window shattered. One of its jagged edges lodged under Starkweather's jacket and lifted him several feet into the air. The debris pile was driven by the water's force toward the hillside, Starkweather riding above it, dangling from the jagged window glass. He managed to grasp a gas pipe that stretched down the slope, holding on for dear life as he slipped from the glass spike. Two men standing on the bank pulled him to safety. Starkweather spent the next several days desperately searching the rubble for his wife.

When Harriett's badly battered and decomposed body was found by recovery workers several days later, her hand was still clutching a bag of jewelry.

— — — — — —

Saturday was traditionally "bath day" in Austin. Madge Nelson, 15-year-old daughter of grocer William Nelson, had just stepped out of the tub in the family's Turner Street home when the warning whistles blew. Madge paid no attention and was drying herself with a towel when she heard the growing roar. She peered out her bedroom window in time to see a train boxcar riding the current, heading straight for her home. Madge instinctively took cover in her bed. She rode for about a half-mile until the mattress landed safely atop a section of the Buffalo and Susquehanna Railroad station ruins that had settled in the mill pond

"I just did what any frightened girl would have done," Madge said. "I jumped into the bed and covered up my head with pillows. I don't remember much more until the bed and I came to a stop. I looked out and did not know where I was. My hair was caught in some debris and I could hardly move. I screamed for my mother, but there was no answer."

William Gilroy, son of Goodyear Avenue grocer Thomas Gilroy, had taken the store's dray up on High Street to escape the flood. After the waters passed, he spotted Madge and hurried down the hillside. Gilroy crawled over the logs floating in the pond to reach the girl. She continued asking about her mother. "She is right here beside me someplace," Madge insisted.

The next day, salvage crews discovered the lifeless body of 43-year-old Mary Nelson—not far from where her daughter had been rescued.

— — — — — —

William Nelson also met his demise in the flood. J. F. Swartwood said he was chatting with Nelson outside of his store when the mill whistle sounded and the two parted company. Witnesses last spotted Nelson dashing for his Turner Street home to rescue his family. His was among the first bodies recovered.

— — — — — —

Mrs. Mina Helwig Elliott and her 16-year-old daughter, Frances (Mrs. Edwin) Erway, were walking into town when they heard the roar of the approaching wave. They had barely ducked into the nearest house when the flood hit. The structure rumbled and was lifted onto the current. Mrs. Elliott reached for her daughter and with their arms clasped around each other they were swept to their deaths.

— — — — — —

Restaurant keeper Martha Kennicut Duell was chatting with a young girl who stopped for a fountain soda when the siren wailed. An excited boy poked his head inside the door, yelling, "Hurry! The dam broke!"

"Oh, let the child finish her glass," said Duell. The boy dashed away and, moments later, the store was leveled and its occupants killed.

———————

Mrs. Laura Erhardt hurried out from her home to the street. She then ran back in to retrieve her handbag, which contained about $20. She had just emerged from her front door when the wall of water and debris hit. The handbag was recovered the following day, but Erhardt's body was never found.

———————

Grace Baldwin Collins, sister of Senator Frank Baldwin, could have easily made it to safety, but she refused to abandon her parents. Mary Murrin, daughter of Town Burgess Michael Murrin, said her mother had called to warn the Baldwins. "Mrs. Collins would not believe her," Miss Murrin said. "But she must have become uneasy, because as I looked back I saw Mrs. Collins leading her blind mother to the door. Then the flood struck the house."

Senator Baldwin was in his Main Street law office when he heard the alarm. "Doubting, I first took up the telephone to verify the information and then, dreading to lose a minute, ran home," the senator said. Baldwin warned his wife in time for her and their children to hurry to safety. He tried to reach his parents' house, but failed, leaving him just enough time to escape. The senator would eventually join in the rescue and recovery operations.

———————

Six-year-old Herbie Reese was sitting on his front porch. His mother stepped outside just as the boy was swept into the waters. She plunged in to save her son. As she tried to catch up to him, a large Hungarian man reached in and plucked her from the rushing water, carrying her to the bank. The panicked mother attempted to break free, but she was held back by several men. As the woman kicked and thrashed, her dress was ripped off and both of her arms were broken. The boy's body was found the next morning.

— — — — — —

Frank Sykes—clothier and brother of merchant Harry Sykes—was busy at his furniture and dry goods store and his wife, Libby, was in bed, having just given birth to the couple's third child. Libby's cousin, Sylvia Miller, was caring for the couple's older boys, Mervine and Gilbert. Harry Sykes suddenly arrived to help them to safety. But Libby hesitated. "I can't take the baby," she cried. "It will catch cold. Wait 'til Frank gets here." Reluctantly, Harry Sykes fled. The other five people perished as the house was crushed and carried away. The infant's body was never found.

— — — — — —

Dr. Edward A. Mansuy had just arrived at the hillside hospital to make his Saturday afternoon rounds. "I did not pay any attention to the whistles until I heard people scream. I then went to the balcony and saw the water. I ran for my home in a sort of half-daze. I could not tell where my home had been. I went to the farther side of the valley to see if my wife and child had been saved."

He spent the night not knowing what had happened to his family. However, early Sunday morning the doctor was present when the body of his wife, Mary Theresa Mansuy, was pulled from the pond of the Goodyear Lumber Company, just a quarter-mile away from where their home had stood. "She was denuded," the doctor said. "I thought she was Frank Sykes' wife and I stayed a while and went in the morgue and could not recognize her. She was not over two-thirds of her ordinary length. She had been crushed all together and was badly mutilated. Later on I went and asked again to see her. I saw three rings on her finger. The first was a miniature signet ring and my photo was in the ring."

The body of his daughter, 10-month-old Ellan Eloise Mansuy, was found three days later. When the alarm sounded, his wife had gathered up the baby and fled out the back door of the house, but the five-strand barbed wire fence caught her dress. When she realized she could not make it, Mrs. Mansuy dropped back to the ground clasping her baby in her arms, turned her back on the rushing waters and was gone.

Two of Frank and Golda Rosenbloom's daughters, Ida and Sarah, looked on in horror from the family's home on the western hillside as Mary Mansuy and four other women struggled to climb over the barbed wire. The girls started down the hillside to help. "Please come back!" screamed their five-year-old sister, Helen. "I don't want you to die." Recognizing they would never make it, the sisters turned back and returned to the safety of their porch, where the family huddled, weeping.

— — — — — —

Olive McKinney collapsed from exhaustion as she carried her three-year-old son up the hill. An unidentified man reached out and snatched the child from her arms just before the water carried her away.

— — — — — —

William D. Robertson, a professional photographer and night watchman for the Bayless mill, had curled up on the couch of his third-story studio at the Starkweather Building. The last thing he remembered was stepping out on the balcony. Robertson must have jumped—a feat that seemed impossible to anyone trying to reconstruct his movements—and ended up on a bridge which had formed near the ground by two wedged timbers. Then he grabbed a tree and held on until he was rescued. No one recognized him until nurses cleaned his face of mud and blood.

— — — — — —

James Lehman, a night shift worker, was also sleeping when the wave crashed into his house and lifted his mattress from its frame. Riding the crest into town, Lehman caught the attention of two men who had taken refuge atop a roof on the south side of Main Street. Irishman Charles Spearing and candy store owner George Horton had climbed the fire escape. Horton was a conspicuous figure as he stood on the rooftop in his white uniform and chef's cap. As the mattress drifted within reach, the men pulled Lehman onto the roof.

Initially, they didn't recognize Lehman, who was too shocked to speak. To settle him, Spearing reached into his hip pocket and pulled out a flask of whiskey, which he started to empty down Lehman's throat. A strict Prohibitionist, Lehman bounded to his feet and stood, in his nightshirt, cursing his rescuers.

— — — — — —

Mr. and Mrs. Jay Gallup were in their store on Main Street when the whistle blew. They stepped out onto the street, expecting to see a fire, but heard the roaring of the advancing flood and the crashing of the buildings. "Run to the hill!" Gallup shouted to his wife. Expecting that her husband would follow, she did.

Jay Gallup, who was handicapped, realized he would not be able to make it to the hill, so he started to climb the stairs of the three-story building in an effort to reach the roof and ride out the flood. As he approached his destination, there was a tremendous crash as the wreckage struck the building. While the structure swayed, the skylight fell and Gallup climbed through the opening onto the roof.

Meanwhile, Frank Robinson, a one-armed stenographer, was on the third story of the nearby Starkweather building when the floor gave way beneath him and the building toppled into the street. Robinson was hurled through a window onto the same roof occupied by Gallup. He landed just a few feet away. Although Robinson was knocked unconscious and suffered a broken jaw, Gallup was able to revive him. Together, the men waited until the water had subsided and yelled to rescuers, who saved them.

— — — — — —

George Sutton had just returned from Coudersport in his new 1911 Ford and parked it in front of the bank on Main Street. Fortunately, the engine was still warm and started right up. Several panicked residents climbed in. "A wall of water 30 feet high was only about 600 yards away when we started up the hill," Sutton said. "We only had about 30 seconds to spare, so I floored it. When we reached the high ground about 300 yards away, I turned just in time to see the hotel swept away."

— — — — — —

Tom Lawler, a bartender at the Commercial Hotel, was playing with his eight-month old daughter on the second story of the family's Railroad Street home. His wife and another daughter were downstairs. "Without warning, the roof caved in over my head and then floated away," Lawler said. "Instinctively, I grabbed my baby and when I found myself floating along with the wreck of the house, I held her above my head. I caught hold of the side of my house and pushed the baby on it and held on tightly. All around me was a sea of slabs. It was all over in three or four minutes, but it seemed like years. The part of the house I was clinging to was rammed with terrific impact into the hill, where I scrambled ashore with both legs broken."

Lawler lost consciousness, but the crying of his baby led rescuers to him. "The dear little girl was so buried in mud that they scarcely believed she was alive," he said. The bodies of his wife, Margaret Kenealy Lawler, and two-year-old daughter, Agatha, were found downstream.

— — — — — —

E. O. Austin's prominent home in the center of town at Main and Turner streets was carried away and shattered. His daughter, Agnes Austin, was alone in the home and was able to reach the eastern hillside. All of their possessions, including priceless artifacts from the pioneer days, were lost.

— — — — — —

Bayless mill employees John Harvey and Clara Dittenhoffer survived the flood, but found themselves imprisoned behind a brick wall. They spent the night cramped in a small, dark room, partially submerged in cold water as they periodically shouted for help and pounded at the walls with loose bricks. The pair began to chip away at a small breach, digging at it with bricks and fingers and kicking with soaked shoes. They eventually opened a hole through which they continued their shouting. The following morning, rescuers heard the duo and freed them.

— — — — — —

Archer Colegrove, a farmer living in the hills north of Austin, was driving down the road just south of the dam. As he approached the area of the Bayless mill he heard the dam give way and turned to discover the water towering behind him. Colegrove lashed his horses into a wild gallop. A steep roadway on the eastern hillside proved to be his salvation. As he swung his horses up onto the path, the spray of the flood drenched him as the high banks of the mountainside swerved the current away from him.

— — — — — —

South of town, farmer Alfred Edwin "Edd" Earle and his brother Alton had started north from Costello to vote in Austin. They stopped at the Brownlee grist mill to hitch their horse and carriage and were continuing on foot when warned by the frantic Herb Young on his bicycle. The brothers ran back to the Brownlee farm. The Brownlees and Alton Earle were able to escape, but Edd Earle insisted on rescuing his horse. He was crushed as the barn collapsed. "It was a horrible sound, like the falls of Niagara," Alton Earle said. "I saw the barn fall on him and dropped on my knees and prayed. After a time I was either dazed or unconscious but later I prayed all night on the hillside. I prayed that his sins be forgiven, for I realized I would never see him again.

"On Sunday, about a mile down the valley below the Costello schoolhouse, we found my poor brother with his neck broken and caught in the crotch of a tree. We pried him out and strapped him on the buckboard to take the body home. The horror of it all set me nearly crazy and I lost my way, driving all night and constantly praying."

— — — — — —

R. F. Thiele, a farmer living between Austin and Costello, had taken his wife to town when he heard the warning cries. "She was up the street about 200 feet," he said. "I started my team and shouted to her to get in the wagon. As soon as I had picked her up I lashed the team into a gallop for the hill, and when the rig was caught in the water swirl we were able to jump out and get away. The team and wagon were swept away."

— — — — — —

Hugh Hutchinson, station agent of the Buffalo & Susquehanna, got the call from Kathleen Lyons and alerted his daughter Margaret. He was running up Goodyear Street when he saw Edward A. Wilber, a disabled Civil War veteran, making his way slowly toward the hillside. "Can you make the hill?" asked Hutchinson. "I think I can, Hugh," replied the old man. As Hutchinson joined his daughter at a higher point, safe from the water, he looked back in time to see Wilber carried away.

— — — — — —

As soon as telephone operator Lena Binckey poked her head inside the door of the Austin bank and shouted the warning, employees dutifully gathered the money and deposited it in the vault. Cashier Charles D. Judd still had time to rush home and alert his wife. Joining hands, they fled up an alley, climbed the high wire fence and scrambled up the mountain.

— — — — — —

Elias Hooftallen, a night watchman who lived on Rukgaber Street, was asleep as the flood carried his house a block. He didn't awake until it banged against another home and crumpled. Hooftallen, still in his nightclothes, climbed out an opening between the collapsed walls. He rummaged for a pair of trousers, pulled them on, and calmly walked through the mud and piled wood to the hillside hospital, where it was determined that his injuries were not serious.

— — — — — —

Harry Park hunkered down in the corner with his back against the wall and prayed. His home was pushed off its foundation into a neighbor's house, collapsing its roof. A ceiling beam fell on Parks, injuring his leg and trapping him. Nearly 24 hours passed before rescuers found him, alert and still praying. When they determined that a stretcher would not fit between the beams, the rescue team summoned Dr. E. H. Ashcraft, who crawled through a narrow aperture to treat his good friend and stayed by his side until a crew could open a wider passageway.

– – – – – –

Elmer Stump of Bellefonte, a Bell foreman working on the hillside terrace, recognized the importance of restoring phone service. After the flood had passed, Stump headed north on foot, carrying a sub-station set and searching for a telephone trunk line where he could connect it. He eventually tracked down a functional line and phoned the company's regional office in Williamsport to summon help. The first news reports that were flashed to the nation consisted of Stump's observations.

Another Bell employee from Galeton rushed telephone sets to Austin, allowing victims to call family and friends. Margaret Mannion, Bell's chief operator in Coudersport, called every doctor, public official and emergency worker she could reach and urged them to report to Austin.

As soon as they heard about the flood, directors of the Buffalo and Susquehanna and the Pennsylvania Railroad cancelled all scheduled runs and dedicated their trains to bringing relief workers, equipment, medical personnel and supplies to the stricken community.

# 9

## A Living Hell

By 3:30 p.m., the waters of Freeman Run had reclaimed their valley. They ran at will, bubbling and snaking their way through the wreckage, channeled in new directions, pooling in some areas and gliding over the piled wood and bricks. Survivors stood stunned on the hillsides, peering down through the smoke at a flattened wasteland.

Heavy rains began to fall, but did little to douse the gas-fueled fires. Concrete sidewalks stood on end. Hundreds of cords of wood from the Bayless mill and collapsed homes formed a breastwork 60 feet high across what was left of Main Street. An iron bridge that had spanned Freeman Run on Main Street was washed away, leaving behind only its stone abutments. A massive railroad car still full of paper from the Bayless mill lodged against the pile after traveling more than a mile in the flood. Shreds of clothing were draped on low-hanging branches.

Rescuers negotiated an obstacle course of broken glass, splintered wood and deep pits of water. Efforts to reach those who could be heard moaning, screaming or yelling were aggravated by the deep, muddy muck of the valley not covered by wood or bricks. Dozens of men and a handful of women furiously tore through the ruins, some sobbing or wailing, as burning wood crackled and billowing clouds of white smoke choked them. Some searchers probed the pooled waters for bodies. Temporary bridges were fashioned with stacked stones and planks.

Relief workers formed a bucket brigade to attack the fires and were hampered by, of all things, a water shortage. The town's hydrant system was destroyed and mill ponds were piled with wood and other debris. Volunteers scrounged what water they could find in ditches and puddles to supplement the modest flow from Freeman Run and hillside springs.

An eerie silence pervaded, only to be broken by a scream for help, the wailing of the bereaved or a take-charge call for assistance from a rescue worker. One woman sat on the porch of a hillside home, rocking back and forth. She had not uttered a word since learning that her child was killed. Many other townspeople were in a deep state of shock. George P. Donehoo, a Presbyterian pastor from Coudersport, consoled the bereaved.

---

Austin Police Chief Daniel Baker initially took charge of security. A first wave of outside volunteers came from nearby Coudersport and Galeton. Five physicians jammed into a car from Port Allegany and a carload of nurses followed. Roads to Austin were jammed with carriages, wagons and an occasional motor vehicle. Some rode bicycles and a few walked a dozen miles or more. Anyone reaching the town from the north had to climb over piles of timber and rubbish.

Coordinated rescue attempts were sorely lacking, but a

number of volunteers soon developed an effective way to reach trapped victims. A long, strong rope was fastened to a floor or a roof. A "heave-ho!" sounded for teams of six or more men to use their strength to pull, sometimes causing a heap of wreckage to fall down into the exposed area. The few horses that could be rounded up were put to work pulling at the collapsed buildings. Some of the rescue attempts were a success, but more often than not the volunteers' sobbing or silence told a sadder tale.

Stretchers were fashioned out of planks. Blood stains soaked into the white sheets used to cover the bodies. The long hair that hung over the stretchers identified many of the victims as women. Many victims were unidentifiable, caked with mud, mangled or burned beyond recognition. In some cases, volunteers would carry the body from a scene while grieving family members fell in behind.

One temporary morgue was set up at the schoolhouse for those bodies recovered from Austin's east side. Corpses pulled from the west side were taken to the Odd Fellows Hall, a large frame building on the southeast hillside that became the headquarters for rescue and recovery operations. Those who were recovered alive were carried over the makeshift bridges and up to the hospital, where a team of doctors, nurses and volunteers treated their injuries.

------

Sixteen-year-old Florence Swald, who worked in a Coudersport bakery, hitched a ride with a friend to check on her widowed mother and siblings in Austin. She learned that her older sister, Martha, had died at the Bayless mill. Swald went to the family's home on the hillside just south of the mill. She found her mother lying on the floor in the darkness, unable to speak. The flood waters had torn off the front steps, but spared the house.

------

Young Elsie Lamley peered down into the pyre. The three-year-old had been far up on the hill, collecting chestnuts, when the flood waters hit. She came upon a group of townspeople standing silently.

"My papa is down there," she said. "He was down town after medicine for mama when the water comed."

"Yes and her mama is down there, too," a bystander chimed in.

"I can't find my house now," little Elsie cried.

A big man took her in his arms. "We'll find a new home for you, little girl," he said as he carried her toward the hospital.

------

Coudersport's Western Union telegraph operators were overwhelmed with orders, including appeals to volunteer fire departments in area communities that instantly dispatched men and apparatus to Austin.

Cornelius Buckley, a *North American* newspaper reporter, reasoned that the seven-mile trip to Keating Summit was the fastest option to summon help, but could not locate a vehicle or horse. Buckley spotted a middle-aged man driving down the road in a buggy and ran after him. "For God's sake, let me have your horse to get to Keating Summit to send word for help!" he shouted. The man refused.

"I'll break your neck and take your horse if you don't let me have it," Buckley warned. A woman who witnessed the scrap joined in. "That's right," she called. "Take it, and knock the hell out of him if he don't let you have it."

Buckley did not wait for consent. Unhitching the horse from the buggy, he jumped on and rode off, arriving at the Keating

Summit train station at about 5 o'clock. He was greeted by Pennsylvania Railroad conductor J. V. Conley. "The man was so excited that little could be got out of him," Conley said. "He told us that the dam had burst and that the entire town had been wiped out by the rush of water and flames."

News was wired from Keating Summit to Governor John Tener's office, where it was dispatched to newspapers across the country, and eventually around the world. Tener put out a call for immediate help from doctors, nurses and engineers who lived along the railroad routes. Several of them arrived before daybreak on Sunday.

In the absence of local leaders, respected Coudersport attorney W. F. DuBois hastily assembled a command team on the hospital lawn to develop a strategy for rescue and recovery operations.

Injuries were relatively few. People either escaped the flood or were killed. Dr. E. H. Ashcraft had the horrifying task of inspecting bodies and determining cause of death. The venerable physician would remain on duty at Austin almost non-stop for two weeks. Many of the victims were partially naked, especially women whose dresses were torn from their bodies. There was no time or materials for embalming. Bodies were placed in caskets or boxes which were lined outside for identification or burial.

For every tragic outcome, there was a triumph. Rescue workers who combed through the flattened portion of the Bayless mill discovered a baby girl, only a few months old, wrapped in a blanket and tucked safely between two wooden beams. She was alive, alternating between crying and cooing.

For a stretch several miles south of Austin, a level, lifeless plane was broken only by two primary channels carved through the valley—mute testimonials to the millions of gallons of water. Some houses tilted from the slopes at dangerous angles. An occasional section of wire or a broken pole were all that could be seen of the telephone and telegraph lines, hanging over the twisted rails.

As rain fell and darkness descended, scattered fires lit the sky, rising high above the town to meet the hovering black smoke. Flames were reflected in pools of black water that dotted the valley and flickered on the faces of exhausted rescue workers, drenched in rain and sweat as they called out to anyone who might be trapped. Others with lanterns roamed the streets in desperation or delirium. Women who had lost their children wandered in the darkness, crying their names in the vain hope they would respond. Here and there a broken man stood at the ruins of his home dazed, wondering if the bodies of his family would be found.

All through the long night, the flood-swept district was brilliantly lighted by flames for miles up and down the valley. The mammoth plant of the Standard Wood Company and millions of feet of sawed timber in the Goodyear yards fueled the inferno. Kerosene lamps or candles could be seen through the windows of some homes. Inside, while children slept, adults paced the floors in shock and disbelief. The Odd Fellows Hall was opened for the homeless, and soon it was filled to overflowing. Many Austin residents ended up at the hospital because they had nowhere else to turn.

The *New York Telegram* and the *New York Times* each broke the story in its Saturday evening edition, telling its readers of a death toll numbering 500 or more. The *San Francisco Examiner* doubled the casualties to 1,000. *London Times* picked up the story and, by the time it appeared in *Le Temps* of Paris, the death toll was said to be 2,000.

The *New York Times* reported in its Sunday edition:

*Bodies are found in heaps. At one place twenty bodies were piled up against the stone wall of a building. A gully six feet deep was washed through the centre of the town, extending almost to Costello, and an almost continuous stream of dead is being found along its course.*

*Building after building went down in the swirl of water and the shrieks of the dying were terrible. The scene is without parallel. Children, scarcely able to toddle, weak from lack of food or sleep, wander about in search of their parents. Women mingle frequently in the crowd, some of them crying, others dry-eyed and hollow-cheeked, searching for lost families. But the most pitiful sight of all was the strong men one met at every hand. Many of them had no power to act. They cried, as did the women and children, and in one instance a man who had lost his family and property sat down in the mud and prayed.*

*It is the general belief that some of the missing will never be found. Many were burned in the fire, and others were ground to pieces by the masses of timbers and stone swept by the flood.*

Austin's hometown newspaper, the *Autograph*, would never tell the story of the flood. Its firebrand publisher, Harry Caskey, was asked if he intended to resume publishing. "I just don't have it in me to do it," he replied.

Bayless Superintendent Fred Hamlin joined the response team and volunteered the services of as many of the Bayless employees as he could round up. It's not clear how word of the tragedy reached his bosses, George Bayless and his brother Frank, but a business colleague shared his observations. "Neither of them is physically robust and rugged," he said. "They are sensitive, highly strung men, and the blow nearly killed them. I seriously doubt if they could have traveled to Austin at that time. George Bayless was so utterly prostrated by the event that his condition was such as to cause his medical advisor some anxiety."

# 10

## *Rescue And Recovery*

Command of the scene was assigned to State Health Commissioner Dr. Samuel G. Dixon. A respected medical expert, the 60-year-old Dixon was best known for his work in the prevention of tuberculosis. From his home in suburban Philadelphia Saturday evening, Dixon ordered State Police troopers pulled from local patrol duties and dispatched to Austin. He also assigned two platoons of the Pennsylvania National Guard to Austin, bringing with them a supply of food, overcoats and tents. They arrived by train in the middle of the night.

Sunday dawned with an overhanging veil of fog and smoke. Dozens of people had arrived overnight, including rescue workers, photographers, news reporters, and good Samaritans. Country women from miles around comforted those who had lost loved ones. Some were put to work climbing through the woods and brush for a mile or more to obtain fresh drinking water. Refugees were gathered around campfires, warding off the morning chill. Workers began anew their efforts to mine

107

into the hills of debris. Coffee and sandwiches were available to residents and volunteers at the Odd Fellows Hall.

The first wave of State Police arrived about noon. A second group came by train as far as Costello and hiked the final three miles, since the railroad tracks were wiped out. They were an impressive sight as they marched into town in their gray uniforms.

All roads leading into Austin were clogged with curiosity-seekers and volunteers trying to reach the scene. Hundreds of automobiles and carriages were turned back. About 80 mounted officers, many of them constables from nearby towns, lined the perimeter of the flood zone.

Census-takers John Kelley and O.C. Cochran joined Burgess Mike Murrin in attempting to account for every Austin resident counted in 1910. This was an impossible task, since many people had left town before the flood. Communicating with foreign-speaking families was a challenge. Visitors to town, such as traveling salesmen, were hard to account for, since hotel registries were swept away in the flood.

Rain began to fall around noon and kept up steadily through the afternoon. This thinned the ranks of those who waited outside of town in automobiles, carriages and farm wagons. As the roads turned to mud, some cars slipped into ditches, but horse-drawn wagons got through.

Farmers arrived with supplies of fresh milk. Austin's branch of the Women's Christian Temperance Union set up a relief tent and a train car loaded with about 1,500 blankets sent from the state rolled in from Keating Summit. S. D. Pelham, owner of the downtown Pelham Hotel, fed dozens of people who lost everything and gave them free shelter in his undamaged rooms.

Commissioner Dixon arrived on Sunday night and convened a quick meeting of the Town Council at the Odd Fellows Hall.

A command center was established in the lodge room upstairs. Using a blackboard that stretched the length of the wall, Dixon charted an organizational structure and declared safety of the town's water supply as the top priority.

Few hospital patients required care, so the American Red Cross nurses and physicians who accompanied Dr. Dixon to Austin were put to work dispensing food.

Some townspeople sobbed uncontrollably or raged at the rescuers to work faster. Others were barely able to speak. "Their senses seem to be benumbed and no two tell the story alike," the *Potter Democrat* reported. "The banks of the stream are lined with men and women with careworn faces, who have lost all hope of seeing their loved ones alive. Now they are only waiting, anxiously waiting, and when the report comes to them that another body is found, they madly rush to the morgue, only to be turned away, as the recovered body is not the one they were searching for."

By day's end Sunday, 24 bodies had been recovered. Eighty-six people were still unaccounted for. Baskets filled with chicken, ham and beef sandwiches, milk, eggs, bread and butter were delivered door to door. Those who missed out were directed to the Odd Fellows Hall commissary, where a line began to form. State Police were posted there to keep order. Daily rations were three loaves of bread, two cans of tomatoes and a two-pound can of roast beef for each household.

"It was a curious and pitiful sight to see the men and women who were forced to seek charitable relief," one newspaper reported. "They had yesterday been prosperous and today were left penniless. They sat on the bench in the dark, gloomy hall or formed a line that passed slowly in front of the table to get their rations. Skilled artisans, well-to-do merchants and professional men were reduced to the same level of want. They sat there silent and sad, and every few hours officers had to clear the hall of those who lingered because they had nowhere else to go."

Associated Press flashed its reporters' observations across the nation on its wire, painting a colorful picture punctuated by the sensationalized style of the era. A story titled "Wind Wails a Requiem" is excerpted here:

> *The curtain of night, rung down on the Austin flood scarcely before its victims all had been claimed and its surviving spectators fully realized how great a tragedy the elements of water and fire had enacted, was lifted by dawn today, revealing a ghastly scene of death and destruction.*
>
> *Spectators, many of whom barely escaped being victims, and hundreds of persons from surrounding towns, looked down from the steep this morning to see the wreckage of some 400 houses, a score of business blocks, three churches, several large lumber mills and three mills farther down the river.*
>
> *In Austin, out of the hundreds directly involved in the deluge, hardly a dozen survive. During the night, searching parties with engine headlights, automobile lamps, pine torches and improvised lanterns of every sort poked their way into every pile that was accessible, seeking any who might be alive but scarcely a living person was found. Surrounded by death, men who at first had shuddered at the touch of a dead body, set about indifferently to search mangled forms for papers of identification. One corpse among so many did not seem ghastly.*

*It is thought that when the wreckage is cleared away, it will be found that a large number of dead are children. In this mass, the bodies of the majority of victims are believed tonight to lie mangled and burned. The halves of houses, twisted telephone poles, huge sections of brick wall, trees, and timbers are so interwoven that the rescuers have to fight their way inch by inch.*

*The annihilation of Austin came on a beautiful autumn afternoon. Women were about the streets for their Saturday shopping and these and the merchants who were selling them goods were caught by the flood. Women rocking their babies at home and others preparing their meals were hurled into eternity before they could realize the danger.*

*In a drizzling rain which changed to a beating storm, hundreds of rescuers carried on their work while many hysterical viewed the muddy corpses, anxious to know if any of them were their loved ones. Fires still were burning briskly in some portions of the wreckage this afternoon, although they had been under control several hours.*

*Pillagers had been at work during the night. The firemen and volunteers did effective work in keeping off would-be plunderers. In several cases the guardians had hand to hand conflict with marauders.*

Austin's flood brought out the best, but also the worst, in human nature. Fortune seekers were drawn to the valley by unfounded rumors that the vaults of the Austin bank and safes of several stores had been smashed and their contents spilled out down the valley. Thieves began helping themselves to whatever they could carry out of the wreckage. Watches and rings disappeared from some of the bodies. Cash registers and merchants' stocks were rifled. A temporary courtroom was set up in the schoolhouse, where eight men apprehended while looting the ruins on Sunday were taken before a justice of the peace and jailed.

Commissioner Dixon responded by tightening security. Only Health Department employees, certain public officials and newspaper reporters could enter the flood zone. Troopers were dispatched to Keating Summit to board each incoming train and inform passengers that only those having business in Austin would be able to ride into the town.

Some of the voyeurs were opportunistic photographers whose works were quickly developed and made into post cards. One of them, Foster Studholme from Olean, New York, had 1,000 cards for sale showing ten different views when he opened the doors of his drugstore on Monday. They sold out within hours.

Pennsylvania Railroad distributed free passes to any flood victim who could not afford train fare. Every seat on its long string of coaches was taken. Even the baggage car was crowded with passengers waiting to go to Keating Summit. Some stood outside in the pouring rain, waiting to board. Those inside waited for hours without food.

Crews began pulling away the utility poles, logs, crumbled homes and other wreckage lying on the railroad tracks between Austin and Costello. The job got easier when a steam derrick and a crew of about 100 men arrived, supplied by the Buffalo and Susquehanna Railroad.

President William Howard Taft sent a telegram from Omaha: "I have been shocked and horrified by news of the catastrophe that has befallen your thriving village. I want to express to you my sympathy as an individual and as President of the United States. I am sure the entire nation joins me. Please wire me in Omaha as to the extent of the disaster and as to your needs."

Offers began to pour in from around the country. At the same time, requests for help clogged the lone wire from Austin. The appeal was tempered by the concession that there was no shelter for the laborers unless they came in bunk cars. More than 150 workers from Buffalo arrived by train, equipped with axes, picks and shovels.

At daybreak Monday, a car load of caskets was dropped off at the railroad station. Survivors – many of them women — were lined outside a shack and tent set up by life insurance companies across from the morgue. Among the signs nailed to trees outside was one that read simply, "Inquire Within."

Dixon sent a telegram to the mayors of Pittsburgh, Buffalo and Philadelphia: "Desire about 400 men sent in a bunk train. Please advise what you can do. Work consists of recovering dead bodies from ruins." By day's end, he had confirmation that about 200 were on the way. The commissioner assigned teams to work on restoring safe drinking water, natural gas service, telephones and electricity.

Endicott-Johnson Company donated 600 pairs of shoes. Sister chapters of the Women's Christian Temperance Union sent the Austin affiliate sewing machines along with fabric, needles, patterns and thread to make clothes for children. Citizens in nearby towns sent cash. Residents of Johnstown used the cry "Remember 1889!" to collect money and supplies for Austin. Churches, lodges and other groups sent donations. Ernest P. Bicknell, national director of the American Red Cross, arrived with $15,000 for the victims. Teachers in Coudersport encouraged their students to bring in coins to help the sufferers in Austin. They proudly presented $53.38 to the cause.

Dixon's inexperience and his officious manner aggravated some of the survivors and volunteers. He declared that the tents his group had brought to Austin were to be used exclusively by the homeless, but most of the survivors had already found temporary living arrangements. Thus, many of the tents remained in storage while business owners were forced to leave their merchandise exposed to the elements and the looters.

The commissioner also came under fire when he limited townspeople's access to the valley while waiting for more men from downstate. One newspaper headline screamed, "Give Us Our Dead!"

"I speak for the people of Austin," said a grieving Senator Baldwin. "Pennsylvania owes us the bodies of our loved ones! For 48 hours they have been in the ruins. How much longer will the Commonwealth leave them there? The state should have 1,000 men working here now."

A separate operations base was established in Costello, where about 200 men moved into vacant homes belonging to the Elk Tanning Company. Some of Austin's displaced families and relief workers settled into homes vacated by employees from the Goodyear mill. Neighbors, relatives, friends and community-minded citizens in the Costello, Coudersport and Keating Summit areas opened their homes. Many of those who had friends or relatives outside of the area packed what they could and left.

Fearing an outbreak of typhoid or other water-borne diseases, Dixon ordered his team to post "Contaminated" signs at public supplies. The notices were seen by many locals as overkill and disappeared.

Some looters were turned away by gunfire. When three shots rang out near the paper mill, people assumed someone had shot a looter. In reality, a bull that had been badly injured in the flood was put out of its misery, butchered and taken to the commissary.

A number of those who "found" goods yielded to pressure, or to the voice of their own conscience, and returned the items. Marie Nuschke wrote of one conspicuous family pawing through the ruins of two main street businesses for bedding, linens and other items. The materials, easily identifiable by each store's label, were later seized by police.

Some people who were not in need appeared at the commissary posing as victims. Dixon's team responded by creating a voucher system.

"So many who come to the commissary have nothing at all," reported Miss O'Hallern, a nurse in charge of the distribution. "They are bowed down with grief. Many of them have lost a father, mother, husband, wife or child. They seemed to cling to the hope that a loved one may not be dead, but probably in their hearts they know better. Some of them may be dependent on outside aid all winter. We have potatoes, apples, grapes, canned goods and smoked meats. There is no need of anyone going hungry today, but what of next week or next month? That depends on the charity of the public."

Many of the relief workers were Italian immigrants from Pittsburgh and Philadelphia, being paid a daily salary of $1.75 by the state. It was an awful task—hard work, poor food, cramped sleeping quarters and the stench of decaying bodies. A number of the workers were less than ambitious; some helped themselves to the valuables they discovered. One quartet explained that they felt justified in stealing liquor bottles from the Higgins Brothers store because they could no longer endure the smell of rotting flesh while sober.

A reporter from the *Binghamton Press* finally reached George Bayless late Monday. By then, the company president had targeted a convenient scapegoat: T. Chalkley Hatton. He claimed that Hatton had irresponsibly miscalculated the depth needed to ensure a secure substructure. As evidence, Bayless cited anecdotal reports that the dam's foundation had held firm on the western side, but had yielded on the opposite end, where Hatton failed to have it sufficiently anchored.

Letters written by Bayless to Hatton told a different story.

# 11

## *Austin Is History*

Tuesday's death toll stood at 38. Train cars continued to roll in with food, clothing, blankets, tents, cooking utensils and medical supplies. Some of the articles were more of a nuisance than they were worth. There were piles of dirty, torn apparel, as if people had cleaned house and dumped their rubbish on Austin in the name of charity. "Why the donors could think that the decent but unfortunate people of Austin could be prevailed upon to wear such scarecrow raiment passes understanding," one newspaper editorialized.

But some cities sent quality supplies that were put to immediate use. In a shipment from Johnstown was a complete woman's wardrobe, with this message: "Please give these to some old lady. I have been through a flood myself." One of the aid boxes contained a package of paper dolls, cut from a newspaper. Written on the envelope in a childish scrawl was, "From a little girl to any little girl who has lost her dolls."

A crude network of pipes was cobbled together to bring water from hillside springs to part of the town. Enterprising operators opened makeshift businesses. One dealer who had salvaged a portion of his cigarettes, cigars and chewing tobacco sold out within hours. A merchandiser on Rukgaber Street reached his dilapidated building and began selling small household items, hawking them as souvenirs of the flood.

Several private companies came to Austin's assistance. Pennsylvania Railroad sent a special train with 200 laborers, paying its men $1.60 a day. Goodyear Lumber Company dispatched 100 lumbermen from its Potato Creek Mill.

"We expect to have the ruins cleared by Wednesday night," Dixon announced. "What we need most is food. Please urge the public to send foodstuffs. Two carloads came in this morning, but it will last only today and our reserve is dwindling." The commissioner dispatched emissaries to Smethport with money that he expected would buy 2,000 loaves of bread, but they came back with only 500.

Newspaper reporters walked among the grieving, trying to sniff out stories that would top the competition with their graphic detail and sensationalism. For a time, they were confused by a seemingly inordinate number of clergymen walking amid the ruins. Many of them were actually flood victims clad in clerical garments sent by churches.

A skull so badly charred that neither the gender nor the age could be determined was found downtown and parts of bodies of three victims, burned beyond recognition, were taken from the rubble of the Standard Wood Company. One woman came to the supply tent clutching a thick book of Tennyson poetry and a box half-filled with chocolate powder. "This is all I saved," she said. "I slept Saturday night on the ground with the book for a pillow and this chocolate mixed with cold water is all I have had to eat."

A despondent older man, clad only in a shirt and trousers,

approached a state policeman, asking, "Can't you lend me an overcoat for my wife? I am afraid she will die if I can't get some clothes for her."

"How about yourself?" the officer inquired.

"I just want to borrow a coat for my wife," he replied.

"Here," said the officer, removing his overcoat. "Take that to your wife."

"And here," said another trooper as he removed his coat. "This one's for you."

Father O'Brian from St. Augustine's Roman Catholic Church was without a place of worship, so he conducted mass at a parishioner's home, where he announced that the church's entire congregation was accounted for. He did raise some eyebrows by advising residents to pack up and restart their lives elsewhere. "We need assistance to get some people away from here," he said. "Their means of occupation is gone and they can only exist on charity. Experience has shown that nothing is ever accomplished with a number of destitute people around, and it will be better for everyone if they receive the means of going where they can earn their own livelihood."

An even more pessimistic assessment was made by Charles Goodyear: "Austin will never appear again on the map. The future of the Goodyear mill and its subsequent shutdown point out the unfortunate lot of the little village. The fact that its industries were already so on the decline means that the flood will sound its death knell."

In Binghamton, New York, the *Press and Leader* quoted an unidentified Austin businessman: "This disaster has hurried the end of Austin. But how terrible the end has been. We are paralyzed and we hesitate to go up from this valley and, looking back at our lost homes, plan for the future."

A number of workers were on their last legs by Tuesday

afternoon. Many had not slept nor eaten since the flood. Another large train load of food, warm clothing and shoes was welcomed Tuesday night, at the same time gas service was restored for heating and cooking in some sections of town.

Pennsylvania Governor John K. Tener and his entourage arrived by train. A tall Irishman, Tener was a former professional baseball pitcher who had served as a congressman for two years before becoming governor in January 1911. He promised to investigate the cause of the disaster and hold the guilty parties responsible.

"My heart goes out to these poor people," Tener said. "I am surprised that the list of dead and missing is as low as reported. The state's experience at Johnstown and the destruction of this place demand legislation. I will urge the passage of legislation which will give the state control over not only those dams to be built, but those already built."

The Bayless company sent a $1,500 check for the relief fund and paid funeral and burial expenses for about 30 of the flood's victims. Meanwhile, Frank Bayless on Tuesday shot off a terse Western Union telegraph to Hatton: "Please come to Binghamton at our expense at once. Advise."

Citizens' anger was directed at George Bayless, particularly after Hatton declared the dam would not have broken if Bayless had accepted the engineer's recommendations. Bayless shot back on Tuesday with a press release:

> *Mr. Hatton's recommendations were made with the idea of making repairs to the dam so that the water could be increased to a depth of 50 feet, or so that if it ever became necessary to fill it up the construction would stand the pressure. While we did not need 50 feet of water, we had thought well to*

*provide for it in case of emergency.*

*This improvement was made by blasting out and removing a portion of the spillway, which was done in a manner to insure perfect safety. While certain repairs were made for the purpose, we never attempted to carry 50 feet of water in the enclosure. Ordinarily we carried about 40 feet, which was sufficient to furnish us needed power.*

*Expert engineers will make a scientific investigation at once. That will be the best way in which to ascertain just what did cause the wall to break.*

*In the summertime, during dry seasons, we kept a man at the gate constantly to regulate the amount of water and keep it at a height that was necessary. This man was not stationed there at the time of the accident, as it was past the time that he had usually been employed in that capacity and it was not thought necessary to have him remain there.*

By Wednesday, most people had abandoned hope of finding survivors. Dixon came under fire when he suggested it might be time to torch the ruins in order to remove the stench of rotting human flesh and prevent a health epidemic, even as many bodies remained unrecovered. The commissioner further offended many of the locals when he attempted to appropriate fancy supplies from the Louis Nuschke furniture store for his temporary office. Marie Nuschke recalled the merchant's ire:

"Dixon sent one of his subordinates a-running to Louis Nuschke, whose furniture store was a complete wreck, and demanded 'a fine upholstered chair for the doctor to sit on, a nice carpet for under his feet, and better chairs for all his help.' Angrily, Nuschke said, 'Get me a crane to pull the roof off my smashed furniture and maybe I can find a chair that you will think nice enough for the great doctor to sit on. It may be pretty damp when we find one, since I have no tent in which to keep the stuff I save. As for the carpet, I think it has gone down the river'."

Eventually, Nuschke did provide Dixon with furniture and carpeting, for which the local Austin Relief Association, rather than the state, paid $167.

Potter County District Attorney Harry W. Nelson held a coroner's inquest on Friday. Fred Hamlin, on the advice of his attorney, refused to testify. Nelson pressed on in the court of public opinion, charging that the state had failed to follow up on its orders to Bayless to repair the dam after the January 1910 scare.

"There could be no such thing!" insisted General F. W. Fleitz, vice president of the State Water Supply Commission, in response to the report. "There is not a scrap of paper relating to it in our records." Senator Baldwin backed him up, confirming that dam repairs were performed solely upon the Bayless company's orders, with no involvement of any state authorities.

The death count swelled to 55 on Friday with the discovery of three bodies – those of Libby Sykes; her young son, Gilbert Sykes, and Civil War veteran E. A. Wilbur. Workers also found the charred bones of two young children. There was not a single instance in which a child lost both father and mother, but there were many left with one parent.

Some of the relief workers, disgruntled about their pay and working conditions, staged a work stoppage on Friday. They were persuaded to return to the job with assurances that their complaints would be addressed. The next day, about three dozen of the men once again refused to work. Dixon responded by shipping them back downstate on the next train.

Restoration of rail service to Costello helped to bring supplies and relieve congestion on the Austin to Keating Summit line. This also allowed the wreckage to be taken away for burning.

George Bayless, secluded in his Binghamton office, formally announced that his company would repair and reopen the pulp and paper mill, with the log dam – which survived the flood—providing the water supply. He declared that employees who assisted in recovery and cleanup would be rehired. Bayless also had his attorneys draw up documents that many flood victims signed, waiving their right to sue for damages. Mill employees were sent out into the debris field to gather up what company pulpwood they could find from the stacks that had washed down the valley.

Protestant funeral services were held over the next few weeks at the Swedish Lutheran Church on Costello Avenue, which had escaped major flood damage. Often, as one group of friends and relatives mourned, another group waited outside to do the same as soon as the church was cleared. The funerals would finally conclude with a service held just before Christmas Day for restaurant owner Martha Duell, whose decomposed body was recovered under a pile of logs just south of town.

Austin Town Council gave property owners ten days to salvage material from the ruins, after which time the job would be turned over to wood companies who were willing to pay the community a salvage fee for materials. State Police were ordered to arrest anyone who was seen starting any kind of fire near the wreckage. With much of water system still inoperable, fire insurance companies canceled policies and refunded premiums.

James Higgins continued to search for his office safe. On October 13, two weeks after the flood, he was walking along a hard-beaten path through the debris. Discovering a piece of rusted metal protruding from the silt, he picked up a shattered plank to scrape away the mud. Soon, he recognized it as his safe, complete with its contents of $600 in cash.

The safe from the Bayless mill, containing the company's end-of-month payroll, tumbled down the valley, but was recovered with its contents intact. A number of other shop owners weren't so fortunate. Their safes and cash registers had been emptied, either by thieves or by the force of the flood.

Dixon's teams dismantled operations on Sunday, October 15, and transferred responsibility to the Austin Relief Association. Fourteen remained missing and presumed dead. Dixon issued a summary of the incident with no shortage of praise for his own actions and the state's response. Notably absent was any recognition of the people of Austin. Dixon could not resist a parting shot: "Upon the arrival of our engineers and physicians on Sunday morning, endeavor was made to press the local people into service, but it was soon found that they were so demoralized that they were of little or no use."

Higgins & Brothers was among the first businesses to reopen in one of the brick buildings left standing on Main Street. The company filled its shelves with new supplies of groceries, dry goods and furnishings. Repair work on the Hotel Goodyear made it habitable within a few weeks of the flood.

Damage estimates from the flood were put in the range of $14 million. Bayless Pulp and Paper Company claimed $1 million in losses, including $100,000 for the concrete dam and the earthen structure upstream. The 700,000 cords of pulpwood swelled Bayless's losses. Much of the plant escaped serious damage. The grinding room took the brunt of the attack.

Goodyear Lumber Company's toll would have been greater had its two mills been operating at full capacity. Goodyear declared losses of 15 million board feet of hemlock and hardwood, with an estimated value of $1.5 million. Emporium Lumber Company and Standard Wood Company also claimed heavy losses.

The American Red Cross recorded 321 families and businesses with damages. Between 750 and 900 people were displaced in Austin and Costello. A survey revealed destruction or severe damage to 167 homes, 64 stores, four hotels, five churches, four livery stables, two theaters and five factories, including the Buffalo and Susquehanna railroad shops. Senator Baldwin owned six of the damaged buildings in Austin's business district and at least three dozen houses. About 250 homes were left standing.

Losses in jewelry, photographs, silverware, china, textiles, clothing, furniture, horses and other animals were immeasurable. Some animals not confined made it to safety. The scattered farms south of Austin also suffered heavy losses of cattle, horses, pigs, chickens and fertile topsoil.

A long blast of the Bayless whistle to resume limited production on Saturday, October 14, symbolized hope that order would be restored. George and Frank Bayless sent a crew up Freeman Run to bolster and clean out the log dam. On October 30, school reopened with about half of the students and roughly half of the teachers returning after a month's absence.

President Taft had pledged Washington's support, and a grief-stricken George Helwig was not going to let him forget it. He led a delegation to Washington to testify before a congressional committee assessing requests for federal assistance. Helwig was grieving the loss of his wife, his daughter, a granddaughter and grandson. His property damage included three homes, barns, livestock and household goods.

But the federal government turned a deaf ear to Austin's plight, maintaining that disaster relief was a state and local responsibility. Adding insult to injury, Helwig later learned that he had inherited just a pittance of his late wife's $20,000 estate. During the decade the couple had been separated, she had amassed a small fortune through successful business ventures. The couple had reconciled just before the disaster, but the only legal document was his wife's will, which left a paltry $50 to her widower.

Cora Brooks pleaded guilty in December 1911 to operating a house of prostitution. Many townspeople eagerly signed a petition pleading for leniency, citing Brooks' heroic actions of September 30 and her generosity in taking care of victims after the flood. Judge John Ormerod acquiesced and fined her just $200. Brooks soon left Austin, married and became the mother of three. Her role was rarely mentioned in newspaper stories of the disaster. The *New York Telegram* credited the phone call warning the people of Austin to "Mrs. Harvey Davis." Brooks died in 1943 and is buried in Portville, New York.

Weeks after the flood, Austin's ballot boxes were discovered several miles downstream. The water-soaked contents were dried and counted. Native son Charlie Austin, with strong support in his home town, won a seat on the Potter County Board of Commissioners by a single vote.

The Austin disaster would be brought to public attention in movie theaters across the nation through hastily produced black and white newsreels. The headline, "Where Austin Was," flashed on the cinema screen to introduce crude footage of townspeople roaming in the muddy wasteland amid shattered buildings. Freeman Run could be seen meandering through the ruins, while smoke billowed from wood piles.

A second newsreel, headlined "Children Searching for the Bodies of Their Parents," captured a young boy and girl pulling two-by-fours from a stack of lumber that was once their home. A couple stood helplessly next to a structure that had been moved off its foundation. About a dozen men, many well-dressed with hats and jackets, played tug-o-war with the side of one home.

As his lawyers prepared to defend the firm and its executives against criminal and civil actions, George Bayless focused on rebuilding the mill. He said he'd be moving to Austin after the first of the year and would become active in community affairs. To raise capital, Bayless stockholders voted to issue $300,000 in bonds and sell one of the company's Canadian properties.

As chief executive of the Borough of Austin, Burgess Michael Murrin wrote a letter of appreciation that was distributed to newspapers and organizations that responded to the community's plight:

*I hereby give public expression to the deep feeling of gratitude abiding in all our hearts for the manifold acts of kindness bestowed upon this stricken people since the first hour of our calamity, that fateful afternoon of September 30, when the lives of so many cherished ones were sacrificed, so many bereft of family and home with the savings of years swept away, leaving scores of our people penniless and, but for the noble charity of our neighbors, to suffer for the very necessities of life.*

*To all and every one who opened his or her heart to mourn, hand to help or purse to give, this message is sent. No finer display of the divine attribute of sympathy was ever manifested; no more generous response to the call for help was ever evoked.*

*To the railroads (sometimes called soul-less corporations), we owe a debt of gratitude. The Pennsylvania, the Buffalo & Susquehanna, the Coudersport & Port Allegany, and the Lackawanna, each tendered instant and gratuitous service to relieve the stricken town and to transport the sufferers to distant friends. The Goodyear Lumber Company, the fire departments of neighboring towns and individuals that rushed to our rescue deserve unstinted praise and have our grateful acknowledgment.*

*It was 'a time that tried men's souls' and through it all shone the souls of men (and women) radiant with noble impulse and glowing with unselfish love. May God bless them all.*

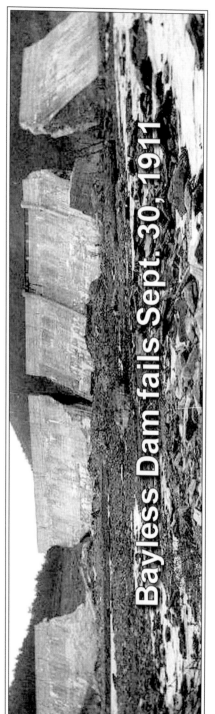

Bayless Dam fails Sept. 30, 1911

Top view looks west from the highway, while the bottom view is from west facing east. Repairs to the dymamited section on the western end had been partially completed and forms were in place for final pour when the dam gave way.

Bayless mill was battered by the onslaught as the flood, pushing before it the stored pulpwood, tore through the plant's eastern side.

Turner St. looking north from Main St. before the flood.

Similar view after the flood; not a house left standing.

Looking northeast. Houses tumbled in heaps along the hill.

Above, before the flood facing southeast. Turner Street at center. So densely populated 'You couldn't a put a house in there,' said one survivor.

**Many stood in stunned silence after the flood waters had passed.**

45

Most buildings on the north side of Main Street were shattered, while many on the south side held their ground. Some victims trapped in the debris were rescued.

The once-thriving Goodyear Mill, which had scaled down its operations by 1911, suffered heavy losses. From an elevated street overlooking the town this view of the mill's south side shows a portion of the debris that piled up in an adjacent pond.

Looking upstream from just below the business district, this was the view from the hill leading up to Goodyear Terrace. On the opposite page, top two photos are from points southeast of Main Street. Below, a man stares at the debris-filled Goodyear pond at the town's west end.

Some structures were saved from total destruction due to their ability to withstand the force or their location just beyond the flood's reach. At left and below, the third-floor 'tower' of town hall overlooks the ruins.

# THE PATH OF THE DESTROYER

As the flood passed through Austin it swept like a wave from one hillside to another, its next target the village of Costello three miles downstream. Because the valley grows wider south of town, the torrent, though still destructive, lost much of its force as it spread out.

**Burning car shops of the Buffalo & Susquehanna Railroad.**

# AUSTIN BEFORE AND AFTER THE FLOOD

A comparison of these images is helpful to anyone trying to gain an appreciation of the devastation. Austin was a thriving community on September 30, 1911, recovering from floods, fires and the rapid demise of the lumber industry. Within minutes, the town was in ruins. Remnants of the Bayless mill can be seen in the distance and buildings left standing on Main Street are evident in the center of the valley.

## TOSSED ABOUT LIKE CORKS

On the opposite page, the lower photo shows the barbed wire fence on the western hillside that prevented several victims from reaching safety. Houses were 'tossed about like corks' as the flood scoured the valley.

These ruins from the Catholic Church had religious significance to some observers.

## Grim Aftermath

Caskets were dropped off beside the railroad tracks. The Odd Fellows Hall became a command center and commissary. At lower right, one of two temporary morgues to which the dead were carried.

Arrival of the destructive force was frozen in time on this Main Street clock found under tons of debris. The 'body' at lower right was probably a hoax staged for a newspaper photographer.

Rescue efforts soon became recovery operations as families gave up hope off finding survivors in the rubble. Below, a stately house came to rest next to the badly damaged bank, post office and telephone building (seen from the rear).

Local volunteers joined forces to search the ruins. Recovery workers, who arrived in droves by train, were served their meals in mess tents below.

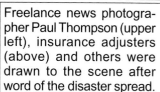

Freelance news photographer Paul Thompson (upper left), insurance adjusters (above) and others were drawn to the scene after word of the disaster spread.

## Horror Sinks In

Helplessness was written on the faces of many victims who survived the flood, but lost most of their possessions. At right, the body of popular Austin grocer William Nelson is transported to one of the temporary morgues. Nelson's warnings of the dam's deterioration went unheeded.

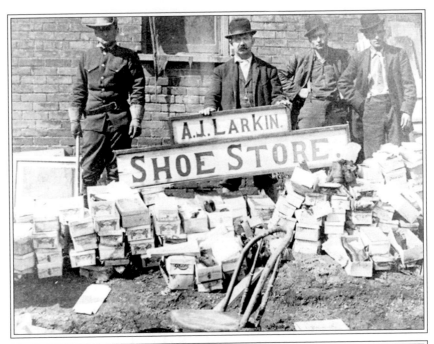

Downtown merchants, including the Nuschkes (above), salvaged what they could and opened for business.

Railroads took a heavy toll as buildings, locomotives, and cars were destroyed and tracks were torn from the ground. Access to Austin from the world was only possible by undamaged rail down the western valley from Keating Summit.

## In the Wreckage

Motor cars were beginning to replace horses for transportation in 1911 Austin, particularly among the more affluent. Many mangled motor vehicles could be found in the valley after the flood moved on.

Above, the water release gate that was initially rejected by Bayless and subsequently installed after the scare of January 1910 can clearly be seen here.

Below, the the Austin Post Office and bank building's damaged section is braced up for repair. The building, looking much as it did then, can be seen today.

## Costello Crippled

Not as hard-hit as Austin, Costello nevertheless suffered much damage. Town's main bridge (top photo) and railroad bridge, above.

Some said Austin would never recover, but many stayed to rebuild. A large community building was constructed in the center of town, paid for largely by the Bayless company.

# LOG CRIB DAM CONTINUED TO SERVE

These rare photographs show the log crib dam that was constructed in 1910 to impound more water and relieve some of the pressure on the concrete dam downstream. Top photo looks north from the dam. Directly above is the view from north to south. At lower left, log dam's bowing caused concern. It gave way (lower right) in the flood of 1942.

# E. O. AUSTIN HOME HISTORICAL SOCIETY

A replica of E. O. Austin's home on the town square, near the original site, is home to a museum celebrating Austin's bygone era.

Margaret Suttton, Author

Gale Largey, Willie Nelson

Dr. Abdul Shakoor

Engineers, writers, researchers and descendants have all been drawn to the story of the Austin flood of 1911. The ruins of the Bayless dam are the focal point of a community park owned and operated by the Austin Dam Memorial Association.

Margaret Crosby

# 12

## Aftermath

Many speculated that Austin would take its place with countless other boom towns across rural America that had faded from the map. Roughly half of the families and business operators left, but those who remained were resolved to rebuild, just as many of them had done after the fires and floods over the past quarter-century.

The Commonwealth of Pennsylvania – for all of Governor Tener's pronouncements – bailed out the Bayless bondholders, but had no financial help for the victims or their families. Austin Relief Association released its final $4,000 to replace sewage pipes, gas and water lines, and fire equipment, and to repair the Costello schoolhouse.

Concrete sidewalks and a brick Main Street helped to usher in new vitality to downtown Austin. A subsidiary, known as Bayless Manufacturing Corporation, was formed to insulate stockholders from any liability claims that might arise from the 1911 flood. Gradually, Bayless built its workforce to nearly the pre-flood levels. The company survived another scare when heavy rains in early April 1912 caused the log dam to overflow. Many Austin residents evacuated. By the following day, water levels receded and life returned to normal.

Bayless was tested by labor strife, equipment sabotage, the employee gutting and instability of World War I, intense market competition, and a fire that damaged a large section of the mill. The company fell into disfavor in Austin when management took a hard line against the employee unions, shutting down the plant for a time and recruiting "scab" laborers when it reopened.

George Bayless, feeling the fervor of the Armistice or perhaps seeking to restore the company's image, diverted attention by announcing an ambitious plan to form a "Patriotic Club," soon renamed the "Community Club." He offered to put up $25,000 toward the estimated $50,000 cost of building a community center, if the town could raise the remainder. Bayless then tapped his own employees to help the town meet its share.

T. Chalkley Hatton went on to become a respected sanitary engineer. He served a term as president of the American Society for Municipal Improvement (forerunner of the American Public Works Association) and became chief engineer of sewage commission for the city of Milwaukee. He died in an early morning car crash on November 11, 1933, at age 73.

Frank Baldwin lost his re-election bid to the Pennsylvania State Senate in 1912, but was returned to office in 1918 and served until he was elected State Auditor General in 1930. He spent his final years in Austin, where he died in 1943. Baldwin is buried in the family plot at Forest Hill Cemetery.

Reminders of the 1911 Austin tragedy surface from time to time. In June 1925, J. J. Wittaker, a farmer in the valley between Austin and Costello, came across human remains while herding his cows. Portions of two leather-tipped shoes were found nearby. By that time, an "official" death count was 79, but seven other people were unaccounted for. Relatives of the missing were contacted and forensic tests revealed that the remains were those of an adult male. A positive identification was never made, but the estimated time of death did coincide with the flood.

Operation of the Bayless plant would always be limited by water shortages. State inspectors ordered the company to place earth and rock fill on both the upstream and downstream faces of the timber dam. An additional spillway was built at the west side, adjacent to the hillside.

The borough's population in the 1920 census was 1,566, scarcely half of the 1910 count. The community center, opened in 1920 at the site of the town founder E. O. Austin's home, was an immediate source of pride. Downstairs, it featured a theater with a raised stage and bowling alley. A large ballroom which was also used for basketball games and roller skating was located upstairs. It served the community until 1972, when it was condemned due to its deteriorating wooden construction.

As time passed, townspeople's bitterness toward George Bayless faded. His redemption came in 1922 when Austin honored him as its Citizen of the Year. Less than a year later, Bayless died of cardiac asthma in his Binghamton home at age 60.

His son, Stanley Bayless, replaced him as manager of the Austin mill. The company weathered the storm of the stock market crash in 1929, but began to scale down production in Austin. By 1931, the mill was operating just three days a week. A decade later, Bayless Pulp and Paper Company, with all of its subsidiaries, sank under the weight of six-figure liabilities, primarily to lumber suppliers, and the economic disruptions of World War II.

To satisfy creditors, the Austin property was sold at an auction on July 31, 1941, Buyer was Veta Mines Inc., a holding company that reopened the plant under the name Williamson Pulp and Paper Company, with Harry K. Williamson as manager.

A series of seven cloudbursts on Saturday, July 18, 1942, sent torrents of water through the region. The timber structure had settled about three feet from its original height and its wooden beams were rotted. The pressure was too much for the dam to handle. When it gave way, upwards of 40 million gallons of water were added to the flash flooding that had already taken a toll in Austin. The current pushed a loaded train of cars and a locomotive before it as it swept through the town. Water stood eight feet deep on Main Street, heavily damaging dozens of homes and many businesses. Tracks of the Baltimore and Ohio railroad, successor to the B&S, were torn from their bed, signaling the end of rail service in Austin. Citizens had time to evacuate the low-lying areas and there were no casualties.

Williamson Pulp and Paper Company, still the town's biggest employer, was seriously damaged. Any hope of the plant returning to full operation was extinguished when fire destroyed the structure on December 23, 1943.

The Borough of Austin and a group of private property owners sought more than $75,000 in damages from Veta Mines Inc. for failure to properly maintain the timber dam. A 1941 state inspection revealing its deficiencies was the key evidence for the plaintiffs. Litigation dragged on for several years. In 1947, a jury in Lycoming County awarded Austin Borough $35,000 for damage to streets. Two years later, jurors ordered the company to pay a total of $72,500 to 12 residents of Austin.

Veta Mines walked away from the property. In January 1953,

H. Brock and Sons, scrap dealers from Coudersport, bought the remains of the plant at a tax sale for $505.

Austin has never fully recovered from losing the paper mill that was its economic lifeblood. A manufacturing plant for the dawning television manufacturing industry, Emporium Specialties, opened in 1948. Foreign competition and marketplace changes have forced the owner to trim operations and adjust his product lines over the years. The business still operates today with a small workforce.

With consolidation of the small one-room schoolhouses across the region, Austin Area School was built in 1953 and five rural schools were closed. It sits on the same flat where two lumber mills once stacked pine, hemlock, cherry and maple 40 feet high. In 1961, the school building was the setting as flood survivors held a homecoming reunion. Among the 150 attending was heroic telephone operator Katherine (Lyons) Dittenhoffer from Cheektowaga, New York.

The dam ruins stood quietly, virtually ignored, in the valley above Austin until 1991, when the Austin Dam Memorial Association bought the property and about 75 acres surrounding it to develop a park. Extension of a dirt road on the western hillside allowed for a different view of the dam and access to a pavilion just downstream from the ruins. In the 1990s, an old 28-millimeter nitrate film newsreel surfaced, depicting the scene in Austin immediately after the flood. Some of that footage was used by historian and videographer Gale Largey, who in 2000 produced a video titled, "The Austin Disaster of 1911: A Chronicle of Human Character."

Treasure hunters occasionally rake through the valley, trying to dig up gold and silver coins, jewelry and souvenirs of the flood. Mountains covered by second- and third-generation timber surround the community. Passers-by see little trace of

## 1911 *The Austin Flood*

the 1911 flood except for the tall, crumbling concrete columns north of town, the focal point of the Austin Dam Memorial Park. Weather and the passage of time have taken their toll. Day by day, the structure is disintegrating, slipping down onto the valley floor. Vegetation sprouts from the loose piles of concrete and stones.

Visitors stop and silently stare in disbelief, seemingly transported back in time. To some, the columns are a graveyard memorializing Austin's quest for a better life—monuments to the working class and a bygone era when a small town bet its future on a man-made panacea. To others, the ruins stand in mute testimony to man's folly, his hunger for prosperity, his underestimation of the power of nature.

Today, Austin is working to secure its future by spotlighting its past. An ambitious plan would draw tourists to a new link between the town and the broken dam through a recreation trail flanked by historical markers recalling the region's rich heritage. Much of that history is recorded in a popular museum established in a replica of E. O. Austin's home on the town square.

Austin has continually demonstrated itself to be a resilient, close-knit community. Its people are respectful of their past and optimistic about their future—their foundation anchored deep in the bedrock of volunteer organizations, churches and small businesses.

And Freeman Run, a century removed from its bondage, flows free.

# Appendix

# A

# *Who's To Blame*

Engineers and other experts all agree that too many corners were cut in construction of the dam. By his penny-pinching stubbornness, George Bayless sabotaged his own dam. Technology of 1909 was sufficiently advanced that a safer dam could have been built.

A more professional and thorough geologic assessment of the Freeman Run valley would have prevented the disaster. The dam was insufficiently anchored. Its foundation should have been taken below the shale layer, where the sliding plane developed, into bedrock.

Bayless's rejection of Hatton's suggested cutoff wall and an accessible release mechanism was the fatal seal. Finally, had the warning signs been heeded and the recommended remedies applied after the dam slid and leaked in January 1910, the structure likely would have survived the late-September rains.

Bayless and Hatton each expressed regret—even remorse—but there are others who bear some of the responsibility.

# 1911 *The Austin Flood*

One newspaper editorialist said Senator Baldwin, while suffering a terrible personal loss, was not blameless: "With his responsibilities both as attorney for the owners of the dam and as a senator from the district; with his 30 houses and business holdings; with his family among the victims, Baldwin was the man who, by position, ability and experience in public service might have been expected more than anyone else to find a way to ward off the danger. Yet, even the leading, pivotal public man in Austin, with all that he had at stake, seems to have taken chances."

Baldwin as much as admitted that he wielded his influence to ward off any dam inspections. He was among the Senators and Representative who felt the wrath of Governor John Tener. "In the aftermath of the Johnstown flood, President Grover Cleveland urged the state to enact regulations to assure the safety of man-made dams," the governor said. "But instead of working in the public interest, legislators played a game of endless political debate. And in the process, they neglected to do what needed to be done."

Pennsylvania was chided by the *Buffalo News* in an editorial: "Even if it were to be shown that there was some kind of State cognizance exercised, the outcome is sufficient proof that nothing worthwhile was done. Now Pennsylvania is to investigate. In other words, Pennsylvania locks the barn after the horse is stolen."

Professional engineering associations were criticized for not insisting on government-imposed dam safety standards, especially after the 1889 Johnstown flood. Thomas P. Rich, a professor of mechanical engineering at Bucknell University, saw a lack of social responsibility:

*Today such a canon for professional behavior is*

*embodied in the engineers' code of ethics, but in the early 1900s, the professional societies viewed these issues to be left solely to the purview of each individual's own conscience and moral compass. With the exception of a very few citizens of Austin, not one of the parties involved with the design, construction or operation of the dam at the local, state or federal levels displayed any sense of social responsibility. These lessons can serve as a reminder to all citizens and societal organizations and institutions of the necessity for constant vigilance in seeking to utilize and monitor technology in ways that are consistent with the public safety and well being.*

Some blamed the people of Austin themselves for failing to demand that Bayless bolster the dam after the 1910 scare. They pointed out that the town had the legal power to seek a court order demanding that the Bayless company remove or repair the dam, or discontinue its use. In an article, titled "A Man-Made Flood," published just two weeks after the flood, Graham Romeyn Taylor wrote:

*Why did not the town government of Austin concern itself with this vital phase of the people's safety? The members of the town council agree that it was never discussed by them officially. Who were the town officers? F. N. Hamlin, superintendent of the Bayless mill, was president of the council. Another member of this body was the master mechanic at the mill. Who was the town burgess? Michael Murrin, superintendent of some outside work for the Bayless mill.*

*Were these men as town officers likely to make a protest about the Bayless company? Austin was a predominantly American community so saturated with dependence upon an outside power from which it drew its livelihood that its very instinct for self-preservation was inhibited.*

Hatton's critics maintain he should have been more insistent on the safety measures and should have shared his reservations with the people of Austin and others. His letters to Bayless suggest that his primary concerns were his own reputation and liability.

Each of the men pointed the finger of blame at the other in numerous newspaper interviews, courtroom testimony and correspondence.

Bayless maintained that he believed the dam would hold until he could build the recommended cut-off wall:

*In building the dam we were guided entirely by the engineer. When the center of the dam slipped, it was evident that the dam did not reach down to bedrock at that spot. Mr. Hatton made two recommendations. He said that we either could draw off all of the water from the dam and on the upstream side, sink a wall 15 feet or so that would reach down to bedrock beyond any question, or we could lower the height of the dam and thereby reduce the pressure on the base.*

*We constructed a dam of logs upstream, to relieve the pressure and provide storage capacity when we drained the lower dam with the intention of building the retaining wall later. We also followed his recommendation by reducing the height of the dam. We felt that the situation was entirely secure and that nothing had been left undone to make the dam entirely safe.*

Hatton emphasized that after he presented his recommendations in February 1910, he had no further connection with the dam:

> *I did not think the company had been using the dam since I had examined it and had pronounced it unsafe. Had the company followed my recommendations, I do not think the dam would have given way. The dam was of good design and was constructed in the best manner possible. The foundation was good solid sandstone. This foundation rock had been undermined, however, by the seeping of water. This caused the damage to the dam a year and a half ago.*
>
> *We made a good test of the rock foundation of the dam before we began to build. We bored through the rock for a distance of eight feet and found no fissures. Eight feet, in our estimation, was deep enough to drill in search for fractures in the rock foundation, even for so large a dam. The fissures must have existed much deeper down, however, for the rock under the dam must have slid, allowing the huge wall to slide forward when the weakening was first noticed.*

The engineer said he was willing to accept some of the blame. "I should have sought the advice of a man more skilled in determining foundations for dams than myself," Hatton lamented. "The great mistake I made was trusting the rock foundation to be impervious. Let the young engineer look to my misfortune. If the frightful fate visited upon Austin results in greater engineering and construction care in dams that are now being built, the sacrifice will not have been in vain."

State Inspector of Dams Alexander R. McKim was alarmed to discover that no cut-off wall had been built upstream from the dam. His official report concluded: "The dam was not being properly bonded to the foundation rock bed beneath, and so a slide followed under the pressure of the water impounded aided by water leakage under the dam. The only anchors were 1-1/2 inch rods every two feet, nine inches along the upstream face. And these were absolutely of no use."

J. W. LeDoux, chief engineer for the City of Philadelphia, analyzed the cause of the dam failure for the American Society of Civil Engineers:

> *This teaches that in building such structures the first requirement is the absolute safety to human life; the second, that it shall serve its purpose; third, that it shall cost a minimum. Apparently, in this case the ends attained were in reverse order. If the foundation is not excavated deep enough the structure will fail, and if it is taken down too deep the cost will be prohibitive, and within these two extremes the engineer has abundant opportunity to tax his judgment to the utmost.*
>
> *How those responsible for the dam could have assumed that it was safe after the January 1910 failure is almost inexplicable. The judgment of the engineer who was in charge of the work at the time the excavation was completed might not be severely*

*censured in view of the accumulated knowledge and state of the art up to that date. It must be remembered that he was working for a corporation who desired to build this dam at the lowest possible cost consistent with safety.*

*The engineer saw the surface of the rock as it was exposed to view, and found that it was clean and hard, and certainly possessed sufficient bearing power to withstand the downward pressure. Therefore, he saw no reason to go deeper, or to believe that the dam would overturn or slide. His reasoning up to that point was absolutely sound, and this would naturally have been sufficient for a great many engineers of standing who desired to save for their employer every possible dollar. Mr. Hatton is an engineer of ability. If he is responsible for this design he went pretty close to the danger point. Still, the course of failure was not due to the design, but to the lack of depth in the rock.*

Other colleagues came to Hatton's defense. J. E. Gibson, a mechanical engineer, observed: "The dam actually failed in 1910 and Mr. Hatton, realizing that he was responsible for the design and would be criticized, did what any of us would have done to correct a piece of defective work. Why the Bayless Pulp and Paper Company did not carry out these recommendations, or at least see to it that the dam was not filled again, is inexplicable."

Lest history judge Hatton too harshly, Potter County historian Bob Currin pointed out that there was little precedent for such a dam and no standardized construction specifications. Currin believes the dam's owner was ultimately responsible:

> *Most sciences, such as geology, were still largely the hobbies of bearded old men and were not taken seriously, but they were gaining respect. The concept of the dam being built in Austin was new, in that the weight of the dam was supposed to the major force keeping it in place. Interestingly, by changing the size, Bayless reduced the weight and anchoring became more critical.*
>
> *It's my opinion that, left to their own judgment, the engineers would have done the job of building a safe dam, but instead they were influenced by penny-pinching management.*

In more recent years, Dr. Abdul Shakoor from Kent State University in Ohio has used the dam ruins as an outdoor classroom for students in his advanced engineering and geology classes. They've studied the subterranean structure and the concrete itself, taking samples back to campus for laboratory analysis. Shakoor describes the study as "a lesson in how not to build a dam."

By 2003, technology had emerged to better assess the cause of dam's failure. Bucknell University doctoral student Emily Monahan created a computer model of the dam and the geology of the valley, confirming the inevitability of water seeping under the structure and causing its slippage. She also built a model that incorporated the measures recommended by engineers Hatton and Wegmann and found that the cutoff wall and added reinforcement would likely have prevented the dam from failing.

Public outrage prompted prosecutors to file criminal charges against Bayless Pulp and Paper Company for involuntary manslaughter. While the case may have pacified the bloodthirsty, it was given little chance of success.

Jurors were first taken to the temporary morgues to view the remains of several flood victims. Court was then convened at the high school, where onlookers crowded into rows of desks and seats.

T. Chalkley Hatton testified that he had opposed raising the height of the dam and had implored Bayless to build the cutoff wall. Hatton also said that he had advised against use of the dam after the January 1910 scare. The jury returned indictments against Bayless and Hamlin, while the dam's gatekeeper, Michael Bailey, was released to testify against the other two.

On the civil side, two opportunistic lawyers pulled together a pool of victims as the Austin-Costello Flood Sufferers Association to file damage claims amounting to more than $2 million against Bayless. Coudersport attorney W. F. DuBois negotiated a settlement. "The company, in my opinion, has done the best that it could possibly do in the matter of settling for the loss," DuBois wrote in a letter to his clients. "I have felt all the time that Mr. Bayless would do, so far as he was able, all that he could to adjust this loss."

Practical considerations—including the threat that Bayless would close the Austin mill for good—provided incentives for the settlement. Each plaintiff received cash and Bayless stock. This had the effect of tying most of the citizens' economic well-being to the financial health of the company.

George Bayless signed off on the agreement with a letter that concluded, "You may be sure that no one feels more deeply or keenly than the writer the loss of life and property incurred, and it is a matter of much regret that full reimbursement is not within our power to command." Removed from the threat of bankruptcy, George and Frank Bayless followed through on their commitment to rebuild, and even expand, the mill.

The long-awaited involuntary manslaughter trial of George Bayless and Fred Hamlin was shifted to Tioga County, after their lawyers argued the defendants could not receive a fair trial locally. The defense team showed that Bayless and Hamlin had reason to believe that the log deflector would relieve enough pressure from the concrete dam to prevent a failure. The heavy rain and excessive runoff had exceeded the capacity of the narrow gate to release water, defense lawyers pointed out. They also presented engineering reports documenting that the defendants could not have known of the specific geologic features that resulted in the dam's sliding. The jury's not guilty verdict, handed down on November 25, 1913, was not unexpected.

Citizens living downstream from the mill sued Bayless for polluting Freeman Run and rendering it useless to people, livestock and wildlife for a distance of several miles. Potter Court records show that the suit was dropped, but no explanation is provided. Soon afterwards, a grand jury indicted Bayless Pulp and Paper Company following a major fish kill. This time, state officials swept down on Bayless and other companies in the region who were fouling rivers and streams. Bayless was among many companies, including tanneries, that agreed to install filtration systems to treat their discharges.

One plaintiff, the feisty Tom Lawler, was alone in insisting that his civil claim be heard by a jury. He had lost his wife and their two-year-old daughter when the family's home was washed away. Jurors ordered the Bayless company to pay Lawler $51,000, half of which went to his lawyer.

George Guncheon was one of the few victims who collected on an insurance claim. His Turner Street house was burning even before it was torn from its foundation and carried away. Because it was painted bright green, it was easily recognizable by witnesses, allowing Guncheon to confirm its demise by fire, rather than flood.

The Austin flood prompted the engineering profession to re-examine its own responsibilities. Engineers began insisting on providing more supervision and inspection, as well as greater say on the selection of sites and materials. Specifically, the 1911 flood prompted engineers to incorporate into their design plans safety techniques such as foundation grouting, cut-off trenches and foundation drains. In 1913, the Pennsylvania Water Obstructions Act was passed, the first dam safety law in the United States, regulating their design, construction and maintenance. The state was given the power to investigate the condition of dams and, if a structure was found to be unsafe, require the owner to repair or remove it.

In 1972, Congress passed the National Dam Inspection Act, which authorized the Army Corps of Engineers to carry out a national program of dam inspections. Between 1978 and 1981, the Corps inspected 749 "high hazard" dams in Pennsylvania. In the ensuing years, the state has worked with the owners to maintain or replace them.

The engineering profession has come a long way, as detailed by Professor P. Aarne Vesiland at Bucknell University:

> *Any profession, be it law or medicine, or engineering, empowers the individual with special talents that benefit the public, and the wise use of these talents for the public good is expected. To do otherwise is to be professionally immoral.*
>
> *An engineer cannot walk away from professional responsibility when the knowledge that the engineer*

*possesses can reduce potential harm to the public. There is, for all of us, regardless of our circumstance or position, the admonition to hold paramount the health, safety, and welfare of the public.*

Dam designers now use computer simulations to more accurately assess structural integrity. However, many of the country's high-risk dams continue to age and inspections are finding new problems. The hazards are compounded by acres of aquifers above the dams being sacrificed to land development, increasing the runoff that flows into impoundments. The National Oceanic and Atmospheric Administration and the National Weather Service are forecasting higher rainfall in the coming years. That, combined with timber clearing that reduces water retention and increased development in the plains below the aging dams, only adds to the danger.

# Appendix
# B

## *Those Who Died*

An exact number of casualties from the Austin flood will forever be elusive. Several bodies were battered or crushed beyond recognition. Some were never found and remain listed as "presumed dead."

A century later, efforts are ongoing by the E. O. Austin Historical Society and others to humanize the victims and go beyond the traditional body count. In doing so, a whole different kind of story emerges – one of lives cut short, families broken, memories lost and so much pain.

In her book, *The Dam That Could Not Break*, Marie Kathern Nuschke listed 78 names in a meticulously documented necrology that has stood as the official count. Victor Beebe, in his *History of Potter County*, cited a figure of 88. Those were, at best, educated guesses. Mrs. Nuschke prefaced her oft-cited summary with this qualifier:

"As near as the author can ascertain, at least eighty people lost their lives from violent death, shock or pneumonia from exposure . . . The Commercial Hotel had one man on the register who was never accounted for. All the people living on School Street out of the path of the flood saw a man run to the top of the high coal trestle that ran between rows of lumber piles on the flat. In a few seconds, the trestle, two cars loaded with coal and the man were rolled into the mass of moving debris."

It's impossible to determine the death toll among visitors. Austin was a popular gathering place for itinerant workers. Because the flood occurred on a Saturday, a busy day for commerce, there were surely out-of-towners in its path.

Some deaths could arguably be classified as flood-related. Typhoid or other bacterially caused epidemics claimed lives, albeit many weeks later.

Following is an alphabetical listing of known fatalities and related information about the victims compiled through the work of Marie Kathern Nuschke, researchers from the E. O. Austin Historical Society and others:

———————————

**BALDWIN, John E.**, 74, handicapped, father of State Senator Frank E. Baldwin; husband of Josephine White Baldwin; Civil War veteran of the 199th Inf. Pa. Volunteers. He and his wife were descended from families that settled in New England before the middle of the 17<sup>th</sup> century. Buried in Forest Hill Cemetery, Austin.

**BALDWIN, Josephine White (Mrs. John E.)**, 64; body never found; mother of Senator Frank E. Baldwin; monument in her memory can be found in Forest Hill Cemetery.

**BARNES, Clarence**, 3; rushing waters tore him from his mother's arms.

**BATEAU, Miss Alice**, 20; Bayless worker trapped amid the machinery of the mill; buried in St. Augustine Cemetery, Costello.

**BEEBE, Mrs. Roxa**, 77; mother of flood victim Adeline Harvey, 55; body found in the ruins near the bank building.

**BENSON, Ellen (Mrs. Andrew)**, 62; last seen entering the Dreamland Theater with her daughter to see the matinee, "Beyond the Divide"; buried in Forest Hill Cemetery.

**BENSON, Ellen Christa**, 9; adopted daughter of flood victim Ellen Benson and Andrew Benson; buried in Forest Hill Cemetery.

**BROADT, Adam, 76**; husband of flood victim Jennie Broadt. The couple lived in the first house below the dam.

**BROADT, Jennie (Mrs. Adam)**, 69.

**BROWN, Mrs. Anna M.**, 33.

**COLLINS, Mrs. Grace (Baldwin)**, 32; sister of Senator Frank Baldwin; wife of M. G. Collins; died trying to save her parents; buried in Forest Hill Cemetery.

**DECKER, Louisa Conklin (Mrs. Jonas)**, 58. Her husband searched for five weeks, often alone, before finding her body, identified by her clothing; buried in Eulalia Cemetery, Coudersport.

**DONOFRIO, Ralph (or Rafilo)**, 33; shoemaker; wife and five children also perished; a burial marker for the whole family can be found in the Costello Catholic Cemetery.

**DONOFRIO, Angelina (Mrs. Ralph)**, 31.

**DONOFRIO, Emma**, 7; never found.

**DONOFRIO, Virginia**, 6; never found.

**DONOFRIO, Monolla**, 5.

**DONOFRIO, Joseph**, 3; never found.

**DONOFRIO, Antonio**, 4 months.

**DUELL, Martha Kinnicut (Moate)**, 44; restaurant keeper; buried in Mix Run Cemetery, Cameron County.

**DUMOHOSKY, Joseph**, 36; gave his life trying to save Olive McKinney and her children.

**DURMIK, Joseph**; died along with his wife and infant daughter.

**DURMIK, Edith or Anna (Mrs. Joseph)**; was rocking her baby to sleep.

**DURMIK, Mary**, infant.

**EARLE, Edwin A.**, 54; went back to save his horses; son of John and Sarah Earle; husband of Carrie.

**ELLIOTT, (Mrs. Frank) Mina Helwig**, 36; daughter of flood victim Hattie Helwig; mother of victim Frances Elliot Erway.

**ENSWORTH, Arthur**, 56; former Potter County District Attorney; body found in the ruins of his office, below Main Street; burial in the Wellsboro Cemetery, Tioga County, Pa.

**ERHARDT, Laura**, 52; turned back to get a handbag of valuables.

**ERWAY, Edwin**, 20; Bayless laborer who slid from the roof of his house trying to grasp his wife.

**ERWAY, Frances (Mrs. Edwin)**, 16, granddaughter of victim Hattie Helwig; daughter of victim Mina Helwig Elliot.

**FILAN, Miss Anna**, 24.

**FITZGERALD, Mrs. Anna**, 60; widow; last seen helping a young child to safety.

**FOSTER, Mrs. Louisa**, 65; bedridden; one of two reported victims of the flood in Costello.

**FUNDATOR, Mrs. Frances**, 24; mother of Edward Fundator.

**FUNDATOR, Edward**, 1.

**GLASPY, Eva Lewis (Mrs. John)**, 48; daughter of Potter County pioneer couple Mr. and Mrs. G. C. Lewis of Odin; school teacher; active in WCTU; buried in Inez Cemetery.

**HARPER, Mrs. Jessie**, 39; mother of victim Jessie Harper; buried at Forest Hill Cemetery, Austin.

**HARPER, Miss Jessie**, 13; buried at Forest Hill Cemetery, Austin.

**HARVEY, Mrs. Adeline**, 55, daughter of Roxa Beebe.

**HELWIG, Hattie (Mrs. George)**, 63; never found; mother of flood victim Mina Helwig Elliot and grandmother of victim Frances Elliot Erway.

**HESS, Mrs. Maggie (Margaret)**, 52; mother of victim William Hess; bodies found together Oct. 7.

**HESS, William**, 23.

**HODGES, Mrs.** (no first name recorded); died in Costello.

**JACKSON, Miss Anna**, 20; originally from Binghamton, New York; in a panic to escape, she fell into a pit at the Bayless mill.

**JUNK, Miss Josephine**, 50; found clutching an 1834 family Bible; identified by a deformity on her ankle; buried in St Andrews Cemetery, Blossburg, Pennsylvania.

**KARPINSKI, Miss Mary**, 22; swept away after helping her mother up the hill.

**LAWLER, Mrs. Margaret Ellen**, 23; mother of flood victim Agatha Lawler; wife of Thomas Lawler, buried in Sacred Heart Cemetery, Wellsville, New York.

**LAWLER, Agatha**, 2; daughter; buried in Sacred Heart Cemetery.

**LOCKWOOD, Mrs. Zadia (Hollenbeck)**, 44; lived with her husband and their eight children in Odin; died on October 1, 1911, from combination of pneumonia and shock; buried in the Hollenbeck Family Cemetery, Hebron Township, Potter County.

**MAGUIRE, Thomas "Tommy,"** 58; Canadian-born carpenter; lived on Railroad Street in Austin; buried in Costello Catholic Cemetery.

**MANSUY, Mrs. Mary (Skelly)**, 29; mother of flood victim Elias Mansuy.

**MANSUY, Ellan Eloise**, 10 months.

**MASCYNSKI, John**, 29; husband of flood victim Mary Mascynski.

**MASCYNSKI, Mary (Mrs. John)**, 26.

**McKINNEY, Olive (Mrs. Joe)**, 42.

**McMANUS, Terrance**, 50; employee of Bayless mill; contracted pneumonia through the exposure and shock and died at the hospital.

**McNAMARA, Joseph**, 3.

**MELTZER, Miss Flossie**, 18; Bayless worker trapped in machinery of the mill; buried in Forest Hill Cemetery.

**MICHELROSKY, Miss Frances** (sometimes used the last name McCloskey), 30; bundler in kindling wood factory.

**MILLER, Edith** (sometimes called Sylvia), 21.

**NELSON, William**, 48, husband of flood victim Mary Nelson.

**NELSON, Mary Kankle (Mrs. William)**, 44.

**PEARSON, Mrs. Mary**, 46; saved two children; dress became entangled in the barbed wire fence.

**REES, Herbert (Herbie) R.**, 6; buried in the Reesville Cemetery in Costello.

**RENNICKS, Mayme K. (Mrs. George)**, 32, mother of seven children, two of whom were killed; buried in Forest Hill Cemetery, Austin.

**RENNICKS, Arnold**, 7, believed to be one of the ten bodies that could not be identified.

**RENNICKS, Evelyn**, 3, found tightly clutched in her mother's arms.

**RITCHIE, Mrs. Lena Graham**, 32. Buried in Forest Hill Cemetery.

**SOFIELD, Mrs. Amelia**, 70; unable to hear the warning due to deafness.

**STARKWEATHER, Mrs. Harriett Moote**, 43; buried in Until the Day Dawns Cemetery, Angelica, New York.

**SWALD, Martha C. (Mrs. Charles)**, 17; Bayless worker trapped amid the machinery of the mill; buried in Eulalia Cemetery, Coudersport.

**SWARTWOOD, Julia A. Losbaugh (Mrs. J. W.)**, 53; buried in Forest Hill Cemetery.

**SYKES, Libby (Mrs. Frank)**, 24; mother of three children killed in the flood.

**SYKES, Gilbert**, 4.

**SYKES, Mervin**, 3.

**SYKES, Joseph**, infant; body never found

**WILBUR, E. A.**; 69, wounded during Civil War; buried in West Hill Cemetery, Galeton.

**WILLETTS, Mrs. Sarah**, 44; cook at Commercial Hotel; often expressed fear that the dam would break.

**WOLCOTT, Louisa (Mrs. Preston)**, 67; long dress became caught in the barbed wire fence.

## *Notes*

A "Harry Maziuski" is shown on some of the lists of fatalities, but no one remembers him. One newspaper account tells of an Antonio and Stella Dilicixo who were married in Austin just hours before the flood. According to the story, he was downtown and was swept away, while she was on the hill and escaped. His body was found on Sunday. She was informed of his death and, a few hours later, her body was found in the rear of a barn near the morgue, the victim of a self-inflicted gunshot wound.

**1911** *The Austin Flood*

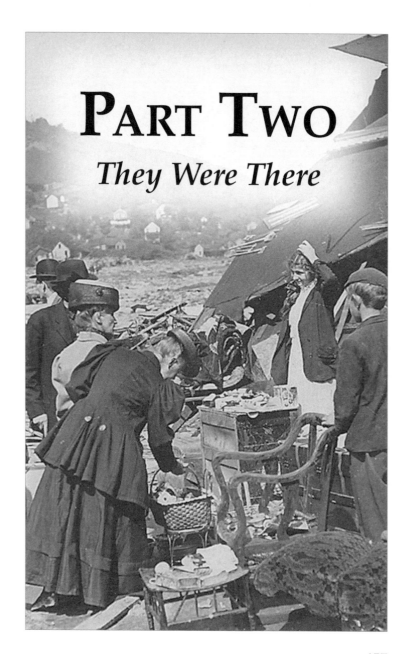

# PART TWO
## *They Were There*

**1911**  *The Austin Flood*

# *They Were There*

Witnesses shared their memories from the Austin flood with newspaper reporters, interviewers, archivists, researchers and others. In the following pages, recollections from some 38 eyewitnesses are shared. Some of the interviews were conducted by the author and other journalists in the preparation of "Flood of Memories," a publication by the *Potter County Leader* to commemorate the 75th anniversary of the flood in 1986. In some cases, the reminiscences represent a compilation of multiple interviews, courtroom testimony and/or writings of the witnesses. Edits have been made to eliminate duplication and keep the accounts focused on the dam, the flood and related topics.

# Clarence Tyler

*(Clarence "Ed" Tyler was foreman on the construction of the timber/stone dam and was able to witness the concrete dam's failure from the north.)*

I was about 40 feet from the road and 20 feet from the east end of the dam. I heard an explosion behind me that sounded like dynamite and turned around quickly. I looked down over the pond toward the dam. The pond was smooth without any real riffles and the wall looked level and unbroken. Then I saw a spray shoot out from the west side of the dam as high as the trees on the west bank. It also flowed out towards the east.

Immediately I saw a wave. It looked like a little white cap. It was rolling rapidly and coming from the west side of the dam. It appeared like a half-circle and was rolling toward the east side of the pond but it only got a short ways when it disappeared and the water in the pond flowed rapidly toward the west side, where the first break was, like it was sloped that way.

I kept working my way up toward the road on the east side to get a better elevation. I was about 20 feet from the road when I saw a backlash in the water from the pond. It flowed rapidly toward the dam which up to that time as far as I could see still presented a straight unbroken line. The water engulfed it, rose up and passed over it. That wave stood only a moment and then dropped back.

Then pieces slowly moved, making a dull grinding sound which could be heard above the rush of the water.

I had a bicycle and when I reached the dam wall, the concrete blocks stood as they are now. The water was pouring through the openings and the pond was all of two-thirds empty.

# L. B. Seibert

*(A Coudersport attorney, Seibert and Fred Keck were riding by the dam with a horse and buggy on the eastern hillside and witnessed the collapse.)*

As near as possible for me to determine, we were a little better than halfway between the pulp mill and the dam at 2:20 pm. I was driving directly toward the dam. I noticed that the dam, which I had not seen for a long time, was leaking considerably along through different places, two or three different places.

They were not large leaks, but the water seemed to be leaking through the seams up and down the dam, perpendicularly. It attracted my attention. I couldn't keep my eyes off it.

Suddenly, Fred said the dam was breaking. He said, "My God, there goes the dam!"

The water was spurting out about what seemed to be three or four feet from the ground and coming through a large hole there that had been broken out of the dam about 50 feet from the west bank. Almost simultaneously, what appeared to be a piece running 20 feet wide, more or less, fell over and downstream. And then as the water began to pour through there, the dam began to buckle, breaking in pieces of about 30 or 40 feet and swinging them like a gate on a pivot and opening up in less than 30 seconds before the last piece was broken on the right-hand side as you go up. And then, of course, all the water was discharged down through there.

The first flow of water was three feet from the bottom. There was a large amount of water, perhaps six, eight or ten feet in diameter, shooting through almost at the bottom of the dam and then a moment later it fell out in one piece like a tree.

As the dam began to buckle, the water ran close to the east shore, or the right-hand side as you go up Freeman Run. It did not break in the middle, but kept picking pieces off and swinging around like a gate. There were six or eight sections.

I went on through past the dam. I saw the water strike Mr. Broadt's house there. The water took a most peculiar turn, like a swirl, and struck almost to the top of the Broadt house. The water was thrown up in a great wave, fully as high as the house.

# Harry Davis

*(A retired Buffalo and Susquehanna Railroad locomotive engineer, Davis was an eyewitness to the dam's failure and was interviewed within hours of the flood.)*

On September 30, water was running over the spillway at about 46 feet. The gate was shut. There was quite a lot of water leaking out around the gate. They had been gradually allowing the water to rise in the dam, coming up to the gate. Sometime in the night it would rise up and then in the morning they would let it down.

With a sharp report a hole appeared in the west end. In a moment water poured through, and the hole was getting larger. In a minute it was 30 feet wide and extended almost the entire height of the dam. Then there was another report, and it seemed as if the whole structure was giving way.

Before I could tell what was happening the water was tearing down Freeman Run, a wall 50 feet high, and sweeping everything before it.

The sound was deafening. I rushed to the telephone and called Central in Austin. She did not have much time to telephone the alarm, but I think she did her best.

I came down to Austin and it was an awful sight. The water had torn through the place and then fire broke out. Worst of all were the cries of the women and children. You see, most all of the men were at work, and they were at home alone. Some of them rushed to the business section and were caught in the water, for that flood traveled like a race horse. Those not drowned were crushed and others were caught in the flames. It was frightful. Cattle and horses were swept off, and even the sidewalks were torn up. I never imagined there could be such force. And over and above it all were the shrieks of people who could not escape.

# Robert Cransie

*(Employee at the Bayless mill.)*

I was about 100 feet below the dam when it gave way. I saw the wall of water, rushing down upon me, and although it poured over me at least 30 feet high it threw me down to the ground.

Somehow I came battling back up to the top of the twisting, roaring mass and grabbed the branches of a tree as it shot past me. I was rescued while clinging to it that night.

------

# Emory Worth

*(An employee from the Bayless mill who was interviewed from his hospital bed on the day after the flood.)*

The wall of the tying room where I was at work seemed to cave in, and that was the first warning I had of any danger. I could see a kind of haze and I thought a steam pipe had broken.

Then I saw the water coming in with the slab piles behind. I tried to jump out of the side window, but the wall caved outward and I was caught in the gearing. The water rose about me but I held my breath, bobbing up for a breath as it surged back and forth. The slabs churning around bruised me up in bad shape, but I am still here, even if I was beaten nearly to a pulp.

# Grace Murphy

*(Grace Murphy was a stenographer in the offices of the Bayless Paper Mill.)*

With me in the office were Mr. Wiser, a bookkeeper, and Miss Mary Decker, another stenographer. We were talking when the telephone bell rang and Miss Decker answered. This call was from a house located near the dam and the voice of a woman said, "The dam is gone. For God's sake, blow the whistle and run for your life!"

We were terror-stricken. I ran from the office and up the track towards the mill, screaming for someone to blow the whistle. There was not time, however, and the whistle at the mill never sounded the alarm. Miss Decker had followed me up the track and we heard the roar and turned and ran across a bridge and up the side hill.

I was so exhausted that, for the last part of the journey, I crawled on my hands and knees. We barely reached safety in time to escape the water that rushed by just below us, carrying everything before it.

In 15 or 20 minutes the flood had passed and the valley looked like the bed of a river filled with debris.

The mill employed about 223 hands, but many of them were home sleeping, as they were employed on the night shift. At the mill there were four young ladies who drowned, Miss Flossie Meltzer, Annie Jackson, Martha Swald and Alice Bateau.

# Mary Blaitz

*(Employee in the counting room at the Bayless mill.)*

I was busy on my books, when suddenly one of the big pulp grinding stones of the mill lurched through the wall. As I leaped to avoid it, the ceiling caved in and the water followed and passed over me. Rescuers found me later pinned beneath the grinding stone. They tried to release me but failed. The great stone was too big for them to move and I thought I would die there.

"Get an ax and cut off my leg!" I told them, but no man would volunteer. "Cut it off!" I pleaded. "You can stand it if I can." I looked up and saw Joe Venarge, a friend of mine. "You do it, Joe, for me," I pleaded. I was in awful pain and nothing could be worse torture than what I was enduring.

"I, I can't do that, Mary," he said. I asked a big man back of him to do it. He picked up the ax. By the lantern light I saw the blade. I think he chopped it four or five times before they could pry me loose.

------

# Eva French

I heard the alarm while working in the kitchen and my seven-year-old son Tom, thinking it was a fire, started down Turner Street on a run. I was warned the dam had broken and started out to catch Tom, screaming to him all the way. It all seemed like bad dream.

I caught Tom and dragged him to the hill just in time, but

I had no chance to give the warning to the school teacher, Miss Smith, who boarded with us and who was upstairs lying down.

When we reached safety, I turned just in time to see the wing of my house torn from the main part and carried down with the flood. As I stood watching, Miss Smith came to the window and waved at me. I expected every minute to see her go down into the flood but by some miracle the main part of the house stood up and she escaped.

------

# Lettie (Moore) Clark

*(She was 11 years old at the time of the flood. She and her two-year-old brother ran to the safety of a nearby hillside.)*

Our family home was swept away by the flood, but we were warned and were all able to escape. My mother was sick in bed and was placed in a rocking chair and carried to safety.

The whole thing is like a hideous nightmare. I recall watching the recovery of a number of the bodies from the wreckage. I remember seeing the body of one man who was so mangled that they couldn't identify him. I also remember seeing the body of a large, white horse way up in the branches of a tall tree after the flood passed.

# Sam Costa Sr.

*(Interviewed in 1993, at age 84, by Paul Costa and* **Growing Up Italian** *author, Patricia Costa Viglucci.)*

I was born in Costello, where my father worked at the tannery. Shortly thereafter, we moved to Austin, where he went to work at the Bayless Paper Mill, as did many other Italians. They were asked their names and when they gave the Italian name, the foreman would puzzle over the spelling and end up giving the immigrant a new, short, anglicized name. We were lucky that Casta was easy to pronounce and spell.

We lived on Benson Street, on a hill, about a half-mile around the bend of the mill, which produced brown butcher paper. The new concrete dam, everyone agreed, was a beauty. It appeared that nothing could budge it. Some people were nervous. Rumors kept flying that there was something wrong with the construction. But others said even if there were a flood, the water that would reach Main Street would be no more than a few inches deep.

For a couple of weeks before it had been raining. Saturday, September 30, however, there was no rain. In our house on the hillside, Mother was cleaning. From an upstairs window, Mother, hearing the whistle, looked down toward the flats. At the same time, I apparently realized something was amiss and began running down the slope from the neighbor's to get to the bottom of our hilly street, meaning to run up to our house. By the time I'd run the short distance, water from Freeman Run had already flooded the flats. My mother saw me running and then spotted a torrent of water behind me. Running from the upstairs bedroom to the first floor and out the door, my mother saw that the water had overtaken me.

Mother saw me engulfed in a swirling mass of water, logs and other debris from the mill yard, which the dam waters were picking up along the way. She came running down the steep, muddy hill, screaming my name. I can only imagine what kind of fears were going through her head. Rushing into the swirling mass of water and logs, my mother managed to grab my shirttail and pulled me to higher ground.

------

# Madge Nelson

*(Daughter of grocer William Nelson and his wife, Mary. She was interviewed by Gale Largey for his 1999 documentary on the Austin flood.)*

I was 15 years old and we lived on Turner Street. I was sewing in an upstairs room when the flood hit. It took our whole house and carried it way down to the Goodyear mill. I just remember coming to and I was in this pile of wood. I cried, "Help!," and they finally heard me and pulled me out.

My father and my mother were found buried in the ruins, just below Austin. As the men trudged along the tracks with my father's lifeless body, a nearby train whistled, and then it threw out a big plume of smoke. John Brownlee said it was like a special tribute to my father.

When my brother Howard and I found that a lot of stuff in our store was still usable, we decided to give it to the people who had lost everything in the flood. We knew that was what my parents would have done.

Like a lot of the people, Howard and I thought Austin would just become a ghost town—that people would leave the town and there would be nobody to remember. So we had my parents put in a single steel casket and then they were taken by train to Wellsville. And there, they rest in peace, just across the Pennsylvania border.

— — — — — —

# Mrs. E. Harter

*(Wife of Rev. Elmer Harter.)*

I wanted to go for my purse in the kitchen, but my husband grabbed me and the rest and with Herculean strength forced us out of the house. Only 10 seconds after leaving the home, it was destroyed. While in the church yard I fell, but Mr. Harter dragged me out of the water as it was closing in upon us. We all plunged through a hole in the fence and reached the higher bank.

— — — — — —

# Lena Binckey

*(One of three telephone operators on duty in Austin when the call came in from Cora Brooks informing them of dam failure)*

The wall of water seemed 50 feet high. Above it rose a great cloud of spray. Houses were tossed, bumping together, spinning and turning as they fell to pieces or were swept out of my sight. The noise was appalling.

I rang as many phones as I could until I saw the debris coming down the valley. A grim eeriness was above it and the roar was horrifying.

When I fled, there were scores behind me, many of them children. They did not seem to appreciate their danger. Some turned into stores. As I ran to the hillside, I could see houses tossing like corks, bumping against one another, spinning and splintering into pieces. A moment later, the green water buried the houses from my sight.

------

# Louis Ritchie

*(Lost his wife, Lena Ritchie, in the flood.)*

Five minutes before the dam broke I left my home to go vote. It was a walk of about three-quarters of a mile. While I was inside the polling place, the alarm was given and I ran out. It would have been easy to reach the hill west of the post office, but I thought of my wife out there alone in the house.

As I ran up Turner Street, I overtook my daughter, Edora. She was hurrying to tell her mother. I told her to get to the hillside. The water was already coming down the valley.

I ran as I never ran before. When I was 50 yards from my house, the flood struck it. I then turned toward the hillside. How I ever got there, I don't know. The water seemed to roll over me every step of the way.

171

# Eleanor Horn

*(She and her husband, Dr. Elmer Ellsworth Horn,
and their two daughters survived the flood.)*

When we were warned to run, I stepped from the front door. The water was above my knees and there was little hope of reaching the hill back of the house. The young girl who was visiting us suggested that we run upstairs and climb through the bathroom window, which opens on the high ground.

By the time the four of us had squeezed ourselves out of the little window it was just three jumps to safety. Just as we reached a point beyond the danger line the flood swept away the house. As I stood upon the hill watching the wrecked homes floating by, my mind was terribly disturbed over the fate of my daughter Dorothy, who went out driving a short time before the dam broke. It turned out she had crossed to the other side of the valley and had driven toward the dam. Both of us stood upon hills, but on the opposite sides of the valley. It was not until some time after the flood passed that I learned that she was safe.

Our home was carried down Main Street and thrown on top of the bank, where we found it on Sunday. My new muslin curtains, tied back with pink satin ribbons, still hung at some of the windows, which had remained unbroken, and inside the battered shell we found some of our possessions.

# Faith Glaspy

*(Age 12 when the flood hit Austin,*
*claiming the life of her mother, Eva Glaspy.)*

Papa was away to Hulls that day. When we heard the alarm we thought it was a fire. I ran down the street to see where the fire was. A man came up the street and said the dam had broken. I went back and told Mama what he said. She told me to run and she would come. She had her coat on and was standing in the doorway when I left her. That is the last time I ever saw her. We do not know if she ever got out of the house.

------

# W. D. Robertson

*(Night watchman at the Bayless mill.*
*Interviewed from his hospital bed the day after the flood.)*

I rushed out to the balcony at the rear of the apartment and looked up the valley. The houses were coming down on the crest of the flood, bobbing up and down like corks. I was horror-stricken, unable to make a move to save myself.

The entire building lurched forward, and then the balcony plunged into Mr. Starkweather's apartments. I fell two stories with the building and found myself protected by a bridge which had formed by wedged timbers.

Somehow I got free. Realizing I was hurt, I walked toward the hospital, crawling over the piled up slabs to safety. They tell me that I have a broken clavicle and my head is a sight, but you can just bet that I am mighty glad to be alive. I have three little kids in Erie. Thank God they were not here.

# Agnes Murphy

*(Agnes Murphy was interviewed by reporter Suzi Bear of the Potter County Leader in 1986, and again in 1995 by Gale Largey.)*

My mother was down in the valley shopping and my dad was at the barbershop. I came so very close to being caught up in the flood. There was a farmer who came by delivering things and he was going to the grist mill in town. I rode with him as far as the church, and then I got out and said, "Gee, I can't go. I haven't asked my parents."

So I jumped off and I stopped at the home of a little old neighbor lady, Mrs. Williams. The kids always used to help her sew rags for making carpets and stuff. It was just a couple doors from our house.

So I went in there and Johnny Nelson was in the kitchen taking the rust off an old iron bed. About that time, John said, "What would you do, Agnes, if the dam broke?" I said, "I don't know. Run home, I guess." And it wasn't five minutes when the whistle blew and the dam broke.

I thought it was a fire. So I dashed up home and my mother came running up, too. She also thought it was a fire.

We were out in the yard and somebody hollered that the dam had gone. So I said, "Well, we'd better go up higher." And my mother said, "Oh, the water isn't going to come up this high." So, she stayed and I ran up to where the hospital was and I watched the flood come down.

The flood made such a terrible roar and it looked just like a huge cloud, just as white as it could be. It was coming down the valley and was pushing the pulp wood down ahead of it. I watched all the debris go down and it made an awful racket.

174

I stood up on the top of the hill, watching it all going down, crying like a kid. Well, I WAS a kid. But, I am a very tender person and it bothered me to see all these things floating down. I watched the water go by for maybe an hour or so.

I watched Dr. Mansuy come out of the hospital. He had his horse tied to the hitching post, and he was pulling the hair out of his head because he knew he'd lost his wife and baby. He knew he had no chance to go after them.

There was a barbed wire fence in back of the church. It was all cow pasture. Everybody had cows back then. They had that barbed wire fence, and that's what caused the death of some people. They got caught in it.

We didn't have any lights here. The only thing that kept the town lighted was the planing mill and a factory down below our house that caught fire. We didn't have any water or lights for at least a couple of weeks. No gas or anything. It also took out some of the roads.

That farmer that I saw earlier in the day who wanted me to ride with him, he was drowned and the horses were drowned. If I had gone with him, I no doubt would have been drowned, too. They said they thought he would have lived if he'd have just forgot about those horses, but he didn't want them to drown.

It was a real bad day. Then people started coming in and, the next day, it just poured rain. There were so many people coming in and they wanted us to feed them. Different people would stop by and ask if they could get a dinner or something. Here it was, tough enough just to feed yourself. My mother did feed others, though, because we had chickens. We took in some.

Then, of course, we had a lot of looters. And that's when they brought the cops in. That was the first thing that started. Everybody was running down there to see what they could find, sifting through the stores.

William Hess—they called him Gun—used to go around and do laundry for people. His body without any clothes on washed up to the top of our bank. My dad looked over the top of the chicken coop and there was Gun's body, right there.

Nobody knows the roar, the commotion, the terrible noise from that flood—all the water rushing down the valley and all those houses and logs floating.

They had a livery stable uptown. I don't know how many horses were there. They were all drowned. There was no way to bury them. They didn't have machinery like they do today, lifts and such. All they could do was get organized and set fire to them. We smelled burning horse flesh for weeks.

Turner Street—you couldn't have put a house in there because it was so thickly populated. The flood just wiped out Turner Street. There wasn't a house left. It was as flat as it could be.

Then they had Railroad Street and that street up along toward the paper mill and a couple of others. Nobody could imagine, if they hadn't gone through it, what destruction there was.

Mr. Nelson had a grocery store on Main Street. He used to go up every night to check on the dam because he was worried about it. He had riding horses and he'd always take one of them up and look at the dam. He was quite a man, a very fine man.

That night, I went down in the yard to look around and down on the avenue these houses were forced together. One house looked just like a saw had taken the whole front off. And I looked up in the bedroom, and there was Mrs. Libby. She was an old lady. She was standing in the corner, and she was in shock.

So I ran home and I told my father. I said, "Dad, you better go up; Mrs. Libby is up there standing there in the bedroom." So he got up and went out and got someone else to help him. And they brought her down.

— — — — — —

# C. F. Collins

I was on Main Street when I heard the whistles at the mill. The people in the stores, the factory hands and those in their homes rushed into the streets and made for the hills. I think about 10 minutes elapsed between the blowing of the whistles and the destruction in Austin.

The pulpwood between the town and the dam acted as a side wall and prevented the water from being diverted. The stream gained in velocity as it struck Main Street.

I saw dozens who made frantic efforts to free themselves from the timbers and wreckage. Dead bodies floated on the surface and went downstream fast. The water passed within 50 yards of me as I stood on the hill.

I assisted in caring for the injured and in the removal of the dead. Many were so mutilated that they were beyond recognition. Most of the people who lost their lives were caught like rats in a trap.

# L.W. Robins

*(A farmer who lived near Austin.)*

On Saturday afternoon, just before the dam broke, I drove into Austin with a load of potatoes. I was sitting in my wagon when the roar told me of the awful danger. I could have whipped my horses and reached the hill, but as I looked up the street I saw that it was crowded with men and women in panic. Rather than endanger their lives by forcing my horses among them, I leaped from the wagon into the street.

The water was above my ankles. The next minute, I lost consciousness. I don't know what happened. When I recovered my senses I was under a house that was thrown across Main Street in front of the wrecked bank building. The water had passed and I had been dragged out by some men. I was wet and chilled but unhurt.

God only knows by what miracle I escaped with my life. The crowd of men and women in the street, for whose sake I abandoned my team and wagon, must have perished.

# Alice Ries

*(Alice Ries, daughter of Methodist minister Rev. Elmer Ries, was 92 at the time she was interviewed by Gale Largey. She was age 4 at the time of the flood.)*

My dad came running down and told my mother, "Follow me right away!" My mother wanted to stop and get her purse, and he said, "No!"

My father took my brother in one arm and me in the other, and my mother followed him right across the street, up the hill. We got to the top of the hill. The house was gone, and the church was gone. What especially sticks in my mind is the church steeple swirling 'round and 'round in the floodwaters. It just took everything in a very short time.

I remember sleeping in a clothes basket the night after the flood. Everyone went to the home of this friend and there wasn't enough room for kids.

Both my father and mother helped with the relief effort. My father and about six other men tied themselves together. When the water was gone so you could walk, they went across to determine who was there and who was on the other side.

All of our friends and family were concerned that, as a small child, seeing all of these tragedies—broken bodies and mangled bodies and so on—would have a terrible effect on my life. But it didn't, because my father sat down and talked with me and told me that tragedy was a part of life. We couldn't ignore it, we couldn't avoid it, but we couldn't let it affect our whole lives—we had to go on.

In March, we moved away and my parents never took me back. And I never wanted to go back.

# Mrs. W. E. Brady

*(Wife of a downtown merchant.)*

I couldn't keep my mind off of the fear that the dam would break, and my husband and I talked it over countless times. We wanted to get rid of our business here and leave, In fact, we were hoping to do so in another three months. Now we have only the clothes on our backs to show for our 25 years in Austin.

I kept planning just what I would do if the dam broke, and months ago I had my son Stewart cut the wires off the fence at a point between our house and the hillside. I owe my life to that, because I had scarcely crawled through the opening when the flood rushed past.

------

# George Sutton

*(Chief Clerk for the Potter County Board of Commissioners.)*

I was with Lloyd Newton, former prothonotary of Potter County, at the eastern end of Main Street when the alarm sounded. I thought there was a fire and I helped to get out the hose cart. We hauled it to Railroad Street when we discovered there was something far more serious than a fire in progress.

Mr. Newton and I ran to the Commercial Hotel, where my automobile was standing. I tried to crank the machine up, forgetting in my excitement that the sparking plug was in my pocket. Finally, when nearly beside myself, I remembered.

We got underway, across the bridge, and up the hill road just in time. From a point near the hospital I watched the flood sweep down the valley. It was terrifying. It appeared in front to be a moving tide of timber, the water at first not being visible. It moved with a peculiar grinding, chunking sound, half crash and half roar. Because of the debris it was pushing ahead, its speed was slow – not greater than 10 miles an hour — but its force was terrific. The strongest building did not seem to possess the resistance of an eggshell.

— — — — — —

# Matthew Curtis Young

I was in the front of our house in Costello playing along the edge of the road in the dirt. I was only three years old, so what I remember will partly be my own recollection and the experience my parents told me about.

Mother was in the house baking bread and my father was at work at the Emporium Lumber Company mill. Somehow he heard that the dam had let go and he and his brother decided to get down to Costello and warn the people. The men at the mill tried to persuade them to stay, but they grabbed their bicycles and took off.

My father continued on down the road to our house. He picked me up and put me on the bar in front of him. He called to Mother, telling her the dam had broken. Mother gathered up some clothing, a couple loaves of freshly baked bread, locked the house and took off down the railroad tracks for my grandfather's. Father, with me in front of him, took off also, hollering as he went.

We arrived at the barn and Father helped get the horses out. We all ended up on what we called the bench, which was a field back of the house and to get to it you had to climb a hill. When Mother arrived, she came to the fence and crawled through between the wires with the clothing and bread in her arms.

The flood struck Costello. Houses went out, chicken coops, pig pens and anything in the way. It swung where Freeman Run joins Prouty Creek, taking out the road bridge and came down the main creek and took out the railroad bridge, which was about sixty feet from Grandfather's house.

The railroad bridge came to a halt about five hundred feet below its original site. Later, a crew of Italian railroad men came in and worked months putting the bridge back on its foundation.

During the worst part of the flood, my mother turned to my dad and mentioned how quiet it was. He said, "My God, woman, are you deaf?" She WAS deaf for a couple of weeks after the flood. As close as she was to it, the noise was deafening with the roar of water and buildings cracking and breaking apart.

My grandfather's place was hardly scratched. Houses had washed in and protected the barn and that kept the flood from reaching the house.

When we were finally able to go up the road to our house, we couldn't get in the front door. Our yard front and back was piled to the porch roof with everything you could think of, but mostly lumber. I remember so many big orange pumpkins and many other vegetables. Fortunately for us, there was a grove of trees about four houses above our house and this threw the flood away from hitting our place direct.

For years after the flood, the debris was in great piles along the creek below Costello. If you needed anything, that was the place to look—pots, pans, lumber, wagon wheels, wire, chicken fence, tin roofs, and just about anything else.

— — — — —

# Bink Fowler

*(Bink Fowler was 11 years old and at her home in Costello when the dam broke)*

Some boy on a bicycle came down from Austin and he was hollerin' for us to get out. "Get out! The dam is broke!" he shouted. I remember that. We had to skedaddle.

The dam was overflowing because of the rain we had for a couple of weeks. And, of course, it was cracked to begin with. But the paper mill—when it run, it run. If anything needed fixin', the hell with it! They'd let her run anyway. That's what those people felt years ago. They didn't want to spend the money.

What homes the flood didn't take, well, there were quite a few fires. We figured that those folks wanted to get a little insurance money and get the hell out of town.

And the sad part is no one in those families in Austin who lost people got anything for it. They didn't get a dime. Babies— they found babies in that wreckage!

There was one lady, a dressmaker, who got out safely and then remembered she'd left some money in her sewing machine drawer. Of course she wanted it; it was her hard-earned money.

183

So she decided to rush back for the money and the flood got her. In those days, if you got a few dollars, you really took care of it. My dad used to tell me that, years ago, if you didn't work for that almighty dollar, you starved to death. No help. Nowadays, you can get relief.

— — — — — —

# Hazel Carman

*(Hazel Carman was in Costello when the dam broke. She was 15 years old at the time)*

A girlfriend of mine was visiting and we were going over to the general store and the post office for our mail in the afternoon when we met this man running down. He told us the dam had broken. I ran right home and got my mother. She grabbed her pocketbook and shawl and we headed for the hill.

We didn't know how far the water would come and we ran up the hill. We could see the flood from there and it looked just like a big cloud of black smoke, pushing all the buildings in front of it.

It was a terrible day and it was years before it got cleaned up. One house got washed from way up the main road clear down to the railroad bridge.

It's a good thing it was on a Saturday. If it had been on a weekday, probably there would have been a lot more lives lost because the schoolhouse was right there. They never would have gotten all of the children out.

# Jack Cooney

*(Jack Cooney was 11 years old, living in Costello, when the flood hit. He spoke with long-time friends Joseph S. Majot and Joseph A. Majot in 1986.)*

There are a lot of stories coming out of the flood and I know that some of them are true. For one, there was the story of Bill Rees. There was a big livery barn that Tommy Ryan had when the flood came. Well, Bill Rees came out of the woods and he had a few drinks and then went up in the hay mound.

While he was sleeping, the flood came and carried the barn clear down to what we called the wagon bridge. He didn't wake up until the thing was all over. He came out of the barn and he said, "What the hell is going on!?!"

The flood had quite a bit of force left when it hit Costello. It cleaned a lot of Main Street right out. When it hit, my younger brothers and I were playing on the hill. Herb Young came down on his bicycle, yelling "Hit the hills! The dam broke!"

So I grabbed both kids. Mother had just come out of the barn we had across the tracks. I took the kids over with me and told her to get to the hill.

We waited up on the hill and we could hear it coming, just like a loud roar. When it hit the schoolhouse, the bell commenced to ringing. That's something I could never figure out. It took the bottom story right out and set the top story right back down again.

It was about the nicest day you'd ever want to see. The sun was shining and it was just beautiful. My dad was uptown in Austin getting my oldest brother out of the hospital. He had been operated on for a hernia and was supposed to be discharged that day. They were just getting ready to come home

185

## 1911 *The Austin Flood*

when the dam broke.

Dad stood up on the terrace. Doc Mansuy was up there. My dad had to hold him back. His wife and baby were down there, but there was nothing he could do for them or anyone else.

They found a woman up by the bridge behind the tannery and it was an awful thing. They couldn't identify her because her head was gone. All they knew was that it was a woman, probably swept all the way down from Austin.

Old Man Nelson had a store in Austin. He'd tell people, all the time, "That dam ain't gonna last." He raised a real fuss over it and he was after them all the time. When it broke, he went with it. They found his body right above Costello.

There was always talk that the dam could break. A couple of times, there were warnings that it was breaking, but it wasn't. That caused a lot of people to worry. As a matter of fact, when word spread that it really was broken that day, a lot of people figured there was nothing to the story. They didn't go up a hill. That's one of the reasons so many people were killed.

I can remember that night, how it was so dreary. No gas. No lights. My mother had sent me down to Harrison's to get some kerosene. When I got out in the yard, a guy came up from the road and I saw what I assume was a state cop. He nabbed the guy and locked him up in a box car. He must have been a scavenger, or a looter. There was a lot of that.

# Victor Beebe

*(Author of the 1934 book, The History of Potter County.)*

I was a resident of Odin, upstream from the dam, at the time of the flood. My telephone was on a party line of 17 phones. Several people were continually talking over the line, all at one time, and no call could be made through the central office, except by some lucky chance. One woman, I remember, whose husband was peddling produce in Austin, was nearly driven crazy before the news finally reached her that he had escaped, though he lost his horse and wagon.

— — — — — —

# Father P. W. O'Brian

*(Catholic priest serving the St. Augustine's Church)*

Our church on Turner Street was totally destroyed, the people's faith shaken and tested. It was a desperate situation. But as the hours passed, they turned to the undying love of God. They believed it was a miracle when they found an unbroken statue of our Lord and savior, Jesus Christ. They saw it as a message, a sign from God, to always remember that in the wisdom of divine providence, there is a time and a purpose for everything.

# Marie Kathern (Brisbois) Nuschke

*(For upwards of a half-century, Marie Nuschke's chronicle,* **The Dam That Could Not Break***, has been the most complete summary of the Austin flood. An eyewitness, Mrs. Nuschke shared her observations.).*

After the fire whistle blew and people shouted that the dam had broken, I waited on another customer at the store. The delay nearly cost me my life. After the woman left, I walked to the store door and saw the great mass of logs pushing down the ravine. Our store was close to the hill so my escape was easy.

No person who witnessed the flood wants to remember the night that followed it. It continued to rain hard. A heavy mist settled over the valley and through it streaked billowing black smoke, while the bright red lights from the flames pierced it now and then, giving a ghastly color to the faces of the people who continued to walk aimlessly on all the streets. Candles or kerosene oil lamps burned in every house and one could see shadowy forms around them.

My father spent the entire night trying to keep a fire burning in a wood stove that had not been used since 1895. He chopped up everything moveable in and around the house and in our yard. My mother was a highly practical woman, so she insisted that we dig the few remaining vegetables in our little garden, which we did, and she had all of them well cooked before morning.

Mr. and Mrs. Frank McLaughlin, who ran a tailor shop on the Main Street, moved in with us, as their place of business and apartment were lost. Since there was no running water in the house, Frank McLaughlin spent the night carrying water from the Garretson spring at the end of Scoville Street. All night long there was a continuous line of people, both friends and strangers, coming to the door, either to borrow something, buy something, or inquire if we had seen a friend or relative whom they had not located since the flood. Our three bedrooms were so small that we had no extra room for people wanting a place to sleep.

About eleven o'clock that night, four bedraggled and muddy men came into the house and asked to sleep on our living room floor. It was not until the next morning at the breakfast table that we discovered that they were four of the high officials of the B&S Railroad Company.

Some place between Buffalo and Austin, Mr. May, the superintendent of the railroad, had bought himself a pair of rubber boots. He had no woolen socks and had put his boots on over his silk socks. After tramping around for hours after he arrived in Austin, he should have made some effort to remove those boots. He may have tried to take them off that night and when they did not come off easily, he decided to sleep in them. By morning, the combined efforts of six men could not pull those boots; they had to be cut off. He had badly infected feet. It was thirty hours before we were able to get a doctor to the house. As a result, we had a boarder for two months who held open office in our living room and shouted orders to railroad men who came and went from morning to night.

About an hour after midnight, we had a caller who left all of us in tears. When Mother answered the rap on the door, she found Miss Mary Decker, a stenographer in the Bayless Pulp and Paper Company office, in a near state of collapse.

Miss Decker said, simply, "Is my mother here?"

We did not have to answer the question. She could tell from our faces that her mother was not there. Mother insisted that she stay until morning, but she refused. We never saw her again, but we heard that her mother's body was found in the debris days later.

When reflecting upon the various stories that came out of the flood, this one is the strangest of all. The name of the family involved has been forgotten, so I shall refer to the woman as Mrs. C. The husband came into Austin to install some machinery in the paper mill and he with wife and little daughter took an apartment in a house on upper Turner Street.

Two or three weeks after the flood when I was working near the ruins of the Nuschke store, Mrs. C and her little girl came along and sat down for a while. She said, "I bet you think it queer that we do not return to our home, don't you?" I said, "No," although I did admit that it seemed strange, since their home was not in Austin, that she would stay there so long after their apartment had disappeared.

Then she said in a confidential manner, "I'm staying for a reason. The morning of the flood I was washing and I took off my diamond ring and put it in a chocolate cup that belonged to a set that my landlady had in the china closet in her dining room. That ring cost $500 and I am staying, thinking that I may find it."

To me, that was a most fantastic story. I said, "Where are you hunting for it?"

"In the millpond," she said confidently. "You know, I have found out that a lot of Turner Street houses went to pieces in that millpond. Some of our neighbors have found stuff out of their houses over there. If I can find where the house that we were in went to pieces, I will hunt for scraps of china and if I ever find a piece of that chocolate pot, then I will be right on the trail."

Days went by. It began to get real cold. Nearly every day

she would stop and report on her findings. One day she was very excited. She said, "I have found a few pieces of that chocolate pot so now I am really digging hard."

Two days later, she came by and was all dressed in traveling clothes so I knew she was leaving. "I want to show you something," she said and pulled off a glove and I saw the ring. There had been no trouble about identity since the initials of both her husband and herself were engraved inside the ring.

With a big smile on her face, she said, "Wasn't that worth digging for?" She said good-bye and I never saw her again.

One of Austin's most prominent citizens, whom I shall call "Mr. Smith," lost his wife and mother-in-law in the flood. Naturally, he appeared greatly disturbed and worked with the men who were moving debris looking for bodies. Days went past and he could not find where his house went to pieces and the workers did not find the women.

Mr. Smith and a few relatives were staying with a couple, whom I shall call Mr. and Mrs. Brown, who had a nice home and several extra bedrooms. One morning, Mr. Smith announced to the Browns that he was going to get a spiritualist from Buffalo to tell him where he could find the bodies of the women. Everyone knew that the two women had always been interested in spiritualism but Mr. Smith never seemed to be interested in any cult or religion.

Two days later a spiritualist arrived and according to the Browns, "the pow-wowing began." For an hour at a time the family of the deceased and the spiritualist sat in a circle, held hands and swayed back and forth while the spiritualist apparently went into a trance.

When she came out of it, the only information she gave was, "they are under a bridge." This was disconcerting news, since all the bridges for miles had been washed away.

Mrs. Brown became very nervous due to so much pow-wowing so one morning her husband decided to put a stop to it. He politely told Mr. Smith that if the bodies weren't found by the end of the week, then they had to leave his house.

Then came a surprise. Mr. Smith motioned for Mr. Brown to follow him into the pantry where he closed the door and whispered, "I am more interested in getting my wife's pocketbook than her body. You may not know this, but I wear a glass eye. I have an extra glass eye that cost me a lot of money and the morning of the flood I was wearing the old one and the good one is in my wife's purse. Also, you know that she had more diamonds than any other woman in Austin so if she left the house, and I have proof she did, she will have the pocketbook full of diamonds and my good glass eye"

Luck was with Mr. Smith. Before the end of the week, the bodies of the two women were found in the millpond; not under any bridge.

Smith hurried to Brown's house swinging a purse and said to his host and hostess, "Hurrah! I was right! Here is the purse she had in her hand." Excitedly, he opened the soggy bag and spilled the contents out on the table – money, diamonds and one good glass eye.

The next morning the whole family plus two corpses and one spiritualist left Austin and were never heard from again.

# Harry W. Nelson

*(Harry Nelson was Potter County District Attorney. He would eventually bring involuntary manslaughter charges against George Bayless and Fred Hamlin.)*

There had been a severe storm only two days before and water was rising in the streams. Judge Ormerod called me. He said the dam had broken and I had better go to Austin at once. When we reached the top of Jenkins Hill, we could see an immense smoke and knew they had fire also. It proved to be the kindling wood factory burning.

The road was dirt and muddy. When we got to Cora Brooks' place, opposite the dam, we saw how the dam had opened and so it stands today. The road was full of telephone poles, pulpwood and debris, so we walked in over the hill. Part of the Bayless Paper Mill was gone and only the roof lay where that part of the building had been.

The valley between the Bayless plant and Costello Avenue was swept clean, excepting a few houses on a high elevation on the road on the upper end of Austin.

Every brick building on the north side of Main Street was gone. Some of the buildings on the south side of Main Street were gone, except for the Goodyear Hotel, Carlson Hardware and a brick building opposite the new Sharp garage. These buildings acted as a barrier and the street was filled with debris piled high to the top of the buildings still standing.

The next night, Dr. Dixon, the state health officer, and the state constabulary arrived on a special train from Harrisburg. Temporary quarters were set up at the Odd Fellow's Hall and the town put under military control.

As far as who is responsible for this disaster, that will be up

193

to the courts and the jurors to decide, but it's my own position that somebody needs to answer for this terrible tragedy and put things right for the people who are suffering so.

------

# W. L. Pelton

*(W. L. Pelton, from Olean, New York, arrived in Austin just before 8 pm Saturday. He rode with W. W. Walker, whose wife was in Austin at the time of the flood.)*

Their home, being on the hillside, was beyond the reach of the flood, and we found Mrs. Walker safe and well. We found the town in darkness, without water, and with very little food.

When we arrived, the kindling wood factory was burning and this was surrounded by an accumulation of pulp wood. If this wood took fire, the dead in the ruins would be cremated, so the workers labored like fiends to prevent this. The B&S shops were also burning.

We crossed the valley and, looking up, we could see the clean sweep that had been made by the rushing torrent. The scene was an awful one, beyond words to paint. People moved aimlessly about, telling over and over again their pitiful story of loved ones missing and homes gone. Scores of homes were torn open, exposing living rooms, bedrooms, kitchens and so on – an inner glimpse of the home life thrown open to the view of the passerby.

As we left Austin on Sunday morning, people from the country around were coming in droves and the roads were almost blocked with rigs and automobiles. The entire affair was something which those who witnessed it will never forget.

# Kate Burr

*(Kate Burr was a news reporter dispatched*
*to Austin to write eyewitness accounts.)*

The first thing we saw when we arrived at Austin at one o'clock in the morning was the water-damaged B&S passenger car where I was supposed to sleep. It was raining hard and blackness thick as a pall was over everything outside the car. Inside, the light of a trainman's lantern revealed mildewed red velvet seats, soaked with water.

The car was cold and damp as a grave, and the silence was fearful. I had started away with courage to face the worst and bring back from their own lips the story of the survivors, but courage—why it was a thing apart from this isolation from every comfort and convenience.

"You had better come up to the house, ma'am, and sleep. You can't stay here. Mother'll give you a bed." It was the cheery voice of the young trainman who spoke and, knowing that pneumonia was the sentence of that car's punishment, I followed the light of the young fellow's lantern – the only mariner's light in a sea of ink.

When daylight came, I found myself in the house of one of the people saved from the flood, but from the conversation which reached my ears I knew that some member of the family had fallen victim.

"He will help me this morning," said a man's voice. "We had better get the grave ready today, even if we do not bury her 'til tomorrow."

Rob Pearson, they call him, said he was working under one of the big engines in the Bayless pulp mill when the first blast of the whistle echoed down the valley.

"But I paid no attention to the whistle because they had been testing it for a week and it had got to be an old story with us," he said. "The first thing we knew, the water was up to our necks. The man who was working with me jumped from a window and, breaking the glass, got through into a room higher up. He pulled me after him and we dashed for the stairs and got into another story with the water chasing us like mad."

The Pearson family of five are very thankful that the life of husband and father was spared, but death did not pass them by.

"They will dig the grave today for my sister-in-law," said Mrs. Pearson, a stout, motherly looking woman whose face wore that expression which later I found was the Austin face since the holocaust—as if she had just wakened from a horrid dream. "She would have been saved but she couldn't find one of her little girls and went looking for her."

------

# L. J. Reznor

*(A jeweler from the town of Port Allegany
who came to help late Saturday.)*

The citizens who were not drowned outright escaped one death, only to be mashed down under the timbers that followed. The entire scene was lighted up by the fires rapidly destroying every portion of the buildings left above water. We could see men and women struggling wildly in the water, attempting to hold onto floating timber.

Austin is so narrow and hedged in by hills that the water

ran through as though coned in a canal. The rescue work that was being done on Saturday night was only by the light from the burning structures.

— — — — — —

# Thelma Stuckey

I was nine years old when the flood hit. I was on the hill picking blackberries when I heard all the whistles blowing in town. I thought there was a big fire and I went home. It wasn't until sometime that night that we heard about the dam breaking.

The next morning, I sat by the window and counted the cars that went by. We very seldom saw a car, but I think I counted around four hundred that morning.

Sunday afternoon my father took me with him to town to see what it looked like. We got as far as the porch of the bank building. There were two houses leaning on each other, half tipped over, and a third house setting crazily on top of them.

As I was looking, I saw the curtain move back and forth and I told my father. He paid no attention, so I took hold of his sleeve to get his attention just as a policeman stepped up to us and said, "Get out of here—your lives are in danger!"

He pointed up there and hanging by a string of mortar, which could have let loose any minute and we could have been dead, was a dozen bricks. I forgot about the curtain. Three days later they found a woman dead with her leg mashed by some heavy furniture in that room.

We started back to where we had tied our horse and met some men carrying a stretcher with a dead woman on it. She had real long red hair and someone told my dad it was the mayor's wife, Mrs. Murrin. We found out later it was not Mrs. Murrin. Everyone was so upset at the time and these men had just guessed and made a mistake.

------

# Ruth Nelson

*(Daughter of grocer William Nelson and his wife, Mary.)*

I was attending college in Williamsport, Pennsylvania. I arrived home Sunday at six in the morning. I had lived in Austin all my life but I had no idea where I was when the train reached there.

We had to get off the train quite a way from the station. There were no lights except lanterns carried by railroad men and it was raining hard. We were taken to a house next door to the post office and bank building.

It was then that I learned that my mother had been found in the debris and that my father had not been seen since the flood. I later went across a foot bridge to another part of the town where my sister, Madge, was staying and we were later joined by my brother, Howard. By this time, we were very sure that our father had not survived. Later, word was received that my father's body had been found.

I have been asked many times why we decided to bury our parents in Wellsville, and the reason was that Mother was born in Wellsville and lived there until she married. My father worked in Wellsville and there he met mother. We had no reason to think that Austin would ever be rebuilt and that of course we had to make decisions hurriedly.

Conditions were very bad. It was several weeks before there was any gas or water, and of course, no stores. My father's store was the only general merchandise place left standing. The front and back walls were gone and the storefront was filled with sand to a depth of over five feet. The sand was a foot deep at the back of the building. As soon as we could get into the building on Sunday, my brother gave to all who needed them many pairs of shoes and all kinds of food that was above the flood level.

Everyone who was entitled to them was given cards for food and clothing. At first I would not use my card, but we had no money. So finally I went to get a little food to help out and it was given to me so ungraciously that I never went but once.

My sister had lost all of her clothing and we went to get something for her and were refused. I later found out that the reason we were refused was that they believed we could buy what we needed. I might add here that my brother had a savings account in one of the Coudersport banks of about fifty dollars and I had ten dollars, which did not go very far towards buying clothes for two people.

I often wondered whatever became of the supplies and money which was sent to Austin. It was quite a number of years after the flood before I found out by reading the report of the Austin Relief Association. The people who lost nothing except their jobs were the ones who received the larger shares and a few people like us who lost everything got almost nothing.

Identification tags were issued to all residents and no one was allowed to pass through town unless they had a tag. One day I forgot mine and the state policeman stopped me. I did not have too much difficulty proving my right to go through and after that he would salute me and smile and wave me on my way. It was not long before all the policemen and workers knew me and the loss we had suffered.

My sister and I had been taught to sew and that winter we were able to make quite a few things, which really helped.

The fact that any people who were in Austin were able to escape was almost a miracle. The loss of life was comparatively small when compared to the extent of the disaster. If the dam had broken at night the loss of life would have been much greater.

------

# Margaret Sutton

*(Author Margaret Sutton, pen name of Rachel Beebe, used her own memories of the 1911 disaster as a backdrop for some of the books in the popular Judy Bolton book series. She was interviewed by the author and by several other researchers.)*

There were so many stories that emerged from the flood that I could have based many more books on it. There are so many ways that a person could interpret the story and identify who was at fault and who should have done something differently.

But it doesn't do a lot of good to look backwards all the time and point fingers because that will never change anything. And besides, as the saying goes, what does a person really know until he walks in the other person's shoes?

That's one of the reasons that I write fiction, is because people who read it are to understand that I am not reporting on anything that happened or placing blame or judging anyone.

Different people are going to have different opinions of who should have done what with the dam, and the scare they had in 1910, and all of the other factors, but whatever you decide about it is not going to bring back the dead or undo the damage. My family lived three miles above the dam. I knew the dam was supposed to be not solid, but I didn't believe it. The dam was beautiful to look at it, and I didn't believe it was dangerous. It looked solid to me. It looked like a lake. It went from one hill to the other.

We were quite shocked to see the town gone, when we finally got down to Austin. It was a shock to an eight-year-old. Even back then, I had in mind that someday I'd write a story about it.

––––––

# Samuel G. Dixon, M.D.

*(Dr. Dixon was State Health Commissioner assigned to supervise many aspects of the rescue and recovery operations at Austin.)*

I arrived Sunday evening in a pouring rain, fully realizing the sad and demoralized condition of affairs. The fire at the kindling wood factory was illuminating the country so that one could see there was little or nothing left of Austin up to the water line along the hillsides.

The following morning, with the aid of Captain Robinson of the Constabulary, an extended inspection was made of the Sinnemahoning Valley, from the dam site to Costello. Parts of houses, trees, iron freight cars smashed to pieces, millions of feet of lumber and pulp wood, bedding, furniture, lumber and stoves, mules, horses, cows and occasionally human bodies were seen strewn for at least a mile and a half below Costello, making a total distance of about six miles.

The mountains above the water flood mark, below which there was nothing but destruction, were covered with hardwoods in the brightest autumn foliage, with a beautiful interspersing of majestic hemlocks. It reminded one of a magnificent decoration with nature's most beautiful leaves forming a wreath around an immense casket filled with death.

It was very evident that the debris covering six miles of the valley would all have to be moved in search of the missing bodies which were buried under lumber, houses, cars and general rubbish. This required an army of men, horses and heavy tackle that the crushed homes might be torn to pieces, and that the cars and masses of tangled timber might be dislodged. All this had to be done immediately, as the bodies were rapidly decomposing and friends were almost frenzied with despair.

Two weeks later, on Sunday noon, October 15, we discharged our last laborers, having turned over every stick in the valley, with the exception of a tangle of material at the Bayless Pulp Mill and two piles at the lumber mills, all of which was being removed by the owners of the materials.

I did my best and left the people of Austin with a heart almost as sad as their own.

# 1911

## *Epilogue*

*Just weeks after the September 30, 1911 flood,
Henry Brigham penned this poem.*

### Austin Town

The peaceful quiet village of Austin lay
In its quiet valley that autumn day.
All unconcerned by the startling fact,
That the dam above had slipped and cracked.
Or of the pulp logs piled below –
God help that town if the dam should go!

And merchants bargained and bought and sold,
With never a doubt that the dam would hold.
And the women laughed and children played,
And none of the villagers were afraid.
For despite the alarms the dam had stood
The test of time and springtime flood,
And the engineer who built it said:
"That dam will stand when you all are dead."

## 1911 *The Austin Flood*

Then a whistle shrieked and the warning shout
Rang through the valley, "The dam's gone out!"
"Fly to the hills! Save who can!"
And men and women and children ran
In wild confusion and mad with fear
Of the awful doom that loomed so near.

For a wall of water was rolling down
That peaceful valley of Austin town,
And licking it clean like the hungry tongue
Of a famished wolf who must feed her young.
While over it all the flood's foul breath
Hung like a pall; 'twas a time of death.

And woe to the child or woman or man
Who stayed their flight or feebly ran.
For the crushing pulp logs beat them down
Right in the streets of Austin town.
And buildings swayed and crushed and fell
'Til Austin town was the pit of hell.

In the peaceful valley of Austin town
Four score were dead when the flood went down.
And vanished and gone was Austin town.
Oh, woe to the engineer who said,
"That dam will stand when you all are dead."

*Many years later, a short poem was written
and shared by Austin's Dixie Ripple:*

# Austin
# and the Dam

Cracked, ruined dam above our town,
Symbol of hope which came crumbling down,
Crusher of dreams not meant to be—
You stand in silent testimony.

A reminder of what was before,
    Broken dam, you are a threat no more.
        You still are there, but so are we—
            Unbroken.

**1911** *The Austin Flood*

*Almost a century after the flood,*
*Carolyn Foster Spano*
*was drawn to the valley:*

I gasp as the weathered concrete dam
comes into view.

It stands, just as it stood a century ago, wounded and
broken—unable to complete the task it was given.
The mistakes of man haunting it with every sunrise
and sunset.

The voices of 78 lost souls whisper through the bare trees.
They are the voices of men, women and children.
The youngest, Antonio Donofrio, a tiny babe of only four
months. The eldest, a 77-year-old, Mrs. Roxa Beebe.
The feeling of loss is all-consuming.

Snowflakes fall silently in reverence, capturing the winter
light as they fall. Fragments of a million prayers float
through the air. I am glad it is gray and snowy.
A sunny day would seem a mockery.

I am overwhelmed, holding my camera in hand, knowing
there is no possible way to capture this emotion on film.
The heaviness in my heart and the chill of the 9-degree air
does not hold me back. The iced surface of the snow
crunches under my feet as I struggle to find the best angle.

But I cannot document
the vastness of my emotion . . .